Original Teachings

Designed to Stand as One

Early Keetoowah
Teachings and Traditions

Also by Crosslin Fields Smith

Stand As One, Spiritual Teachings of Keetoowah, Awakening to the Original Truths

Original Teachings

Designed to Stand as One

Early Keetoowah
Teachings and Traditions

by

Crosslin Fields Smith

Dog Soldier Press
P.O. Box 1782
Ranchos de Taos
New Mexico 87557

Library of Congress Control Number: 2021908528

Printing: Ingram Sparks

Print ISBN: 978-1-7371362-2-4

ePub ISBN: 978-1-7371362-3-1

Editor:

Clint Carroll, Ph.D.
Associate Professor
Department of Ethnic Studies
University of Colorado, Boulder

Cover Art:

Mary HorseChief
Native Connections Director
Cherokee Nation Behavioral Health Prevention
Tahlequah, Oklahoma

Back Cover Photo Credit:

Stokes Smith

Book Design and Layout:

Ananda M. Sundari
AlchemyArts
AlchemyArtsllc.com

ᎠᏂᎦᏴᎵ ᏄᏂᏪᏒᎢ ᎡᎶᎯ ᏛᏛᎦᏂ ᎤᎵᏰᏗᏍᎬᎢ “ᎦᏚᏩᎩ,”
ᎮᏍᏗ ᏱᏅᏩᎨᏫᏏ ᎤᏁᎸᏅᎯ ᏗᏕᏲᏅᎯ.

Anigayvli nuniwesv'i elohi dvtvgani uliyedisgvi "Gaduwagi,"
hesdi yinvwakewsi Unehlvnvhi dideyonvhi.

The Old Ones prophesized that one day the world will hear murmurs of "Keetoowah," lest they forget the Original Teachings of the Creator.

Dedicated to my brother, "Smithy" Ben Smith.
Much of what is written in this book comes from him.

ᎠᏓᎨᏍᏗ ᎾᏂᎠ ᏴᏫ ᏕᏣᏓᎨᏳᏎᏍᏗ ᏂᎦᏗ ᎡᎶᎯ ᏗᎬᏂᏅᎩ.

Adagesdi nani'a yvwi detsadageyusesdi nigadi elohi digvninvgi.

Honor all people with love, even to the last day on this earth.

~ Keetoowah Proverb

In memory of those I have known in my lifetime
who have embraced and modeled this sacred concept,
adagesdi - love and care for oneself and all people:

Benny Smith
Donn F. Baker
Rennard Strickland

The Seven Original Bylaws

1. Love yourself
2. Love me (Creator)
3. Love the Eternal Flame (fire)
4. Love the Earth
5. Love the Air
6. Love the Water
7. Love all humankind

Crosslin Smith in 1985, serving as officiant for a friend's wedding.
Photo credit: Fannie Robinson

Table of Contents

Foreword

ᎣᏏᏲ ᏂᎦᏓ. To be Cherokee is both a great honor and an equally great responsibility. Throughout our history, we have always looked to our revered Elders to guide us in times of prosperity and in times of duress. It is the bravest and most learned of these Elders upon which we bestow the title of National Treasure; it is an elite group and Mr. Crosslin Fields Smith exemplifies this distinction in remarkable ways.

Crosslin is the epitome of what it means to be "Cherokee." He is a warrior, serving the United States Army as a combat soldier in the Korean War and as a technical adviser to this day. He is an educator, committed to teaching Cherokee values and spirituality from preschool to post-doctorate levels. At over ninety years of age, he remains dedicated to preserving traditional practices in our Cherokee communities. He is a spiritual leader, often serving as the conduit for maintaining our culture and traditions in today's modern world. He is a healer, dedicating the majority of his life to alleviate the suffering of his fellow man, with a near constant stream of patients seeking his aid and counsel. He is a Cherokee public servant, one that has served every Cherokee Chief of the modern era, from Keeler to Swimmer to Mankiller to Byrd to Smith to Crittenden to Baker and to myself. It is with great honor and admiration that I receive his wisdom and support as Principal Chief.

Crosslin's gifts are many, yet one that is truly unique is his connection to our past. We Cherokee cannot continue to be Cherokee without following the spiritual guidance of our ancestors. Today, his continued practice and teaching keep us grounded in our culture and guided along the traditional path. He has spent a lifetime shepherding his fellow man, Cherokee and non-Cherokee alike, from a place of deep respect and a unique appreciation of the past, present, and future.

Be it in our darkest times or in instances of our greatest achievement, I, and many Cherokee Chiefs before me, have called upon him to comfort, guide, and encourage Cherokee people wherever they may call home. Upon the death of an eminent Cherokee Elder, I recall Crosslin relaying to us the story of the "Cherokee Seven Heavens," which explains our traditional roles in this world and beyond. Crosslin's ability to unite our Cherokee past with our present day is a source of profound inspiration for our Cherokee communities.

Crosslin's contributions are a gift we can never repay, nor are we likely to ever find another like him. While many refer to Crosslin as a "Medicine Man," that reference does not fully capture his wider role of enlightening all people on the original truths of the Cherokee and our collective history. He is truly the embodiment of the Cherokee way. Even now, he greets each sunrise by gathering the plants and other natural resources for healing and spiritual guidance - a life of sincere Cherokee devotion. In closing, Crosslin is a true Cherokee leader. He is a man with an extraordinary connection to our traditional ways, which he shares along with our culture, to all who seek help and knowledge. I am grateful that my friend and revered Elder is willing to share this book of Cherokee insight and teaching with us and future generations.

GV, Crosslin
Chuck Hoskin Jr., Principal Chief
Cherokee Nation

Prologue

The contents of this book relate to the unwritten bylaws of the traditional Cherokee people known as the Keetoowah Society. They were previously unwritten because Keetoowah people kept the bylaws in their heads and continually lived them. Each day, in all that they did, they kept the bylaws alive. The Creator gave these Original Teachings to *all* people. Racism has no place in them. What I am relating in this book is intended for all humanity.

The reason for writing this book is that I am troubled by the corruption and erosion of respect for humankind and the Earth in the various organizations and institutions of this world. One could easily point out these maladies in many of the political systems throughout the globe, as well as the world's major religious organizations. Such maladies even exist within our Native American communities, whether it be at ceremonial grounds or in Indian churches. In this book, I offer the Original Teachings of Keetoowah to move us all to end conflict with one another, leaving no one out. In ancient times, God told all people that even if there are just three who still follow his Original Instructions, they will be able to help those who have lost sight of them.

Today, it's hard to find three good people in any organization in this world. It parallels the story in the Bible of Sodom and Gomorrah, in which God decided to destroy their city and all the people that lived there because evil had taken over everything. Someone then asked whether

God would spare their city if they could find thirty good people. God answered, saying: Find ten good people and you'll be spared. To me, this story shows that the Creator walked among people, and He still does. He knew that those who retained and lived his Original Teachings were few. Looking at our original spiritual beliefs and practices, I can see that Keetoowah people are among these few; we never became indifferent to those teachings.

This book builds upon my first book, *Stand as One,* to expand on some of the concepts there and to offer new insights from Keetoowah Cherokee teachings. I hope it can show how enacting these teachings might restore goodness and hope in the world.

Chapter 1

Traditions

As a young boy, I remember how the Seven Medicine Men from each of the Cherokee clans used to come together every month at our ceremonial grounds to do a spiritual intercession. This meeting was to encourage all people to do well and get along with one another. As part of their work, the Seven Medicine Men also prepared spiritual medicine for our warriors. The Keetoowah Society has a record of 2,000 of our traditional men who carried this medicine to war, including World Wars I and II. These men did not get hurt. Some might wonder: how is this possible? The explanation is that our spiritual medicine, according to the Original Teachings, begins with honoring all people in all that we do. In preparing the medicine for our warriors, the Seven Medicine Men included all people in their prayers. They believed in all people. This was a Creator-given concept that they practiced. It was strong medicine, and it was backed by this spiritual power because it acknowledged all humanity and all life.

Our history tells of a time when people became indifferent and stopped praying to the Creator. Instead, they began praying to idols. This created a space for the Son of God to come into the picture to teach and remind people of these concepts. But the Brown People, who were at that time one group of people - one tribe - had not become indifferent. They continued to live by the Creator's teachings of **love** and **spirit**, which declare a profound love for all humankind and acknowledge the original Spirit that resides within us and has been given to all people by the Creator. These are the original gifts to all mankind. They are precious. When you live by these concepts, you satisfy both the teachings of the Creator and the concepts expressed in the Bible.

Our legends and stories recount how we have lived in three previous worlds, or eras. Keetoowah teachings speak of our ancient origins in what is called the First World, and that this time ended with a migration that resulted from a great flood. The beginning of what is called the Second World occurred when our ancestors arrived on an island at the end of this journey. This island is said to have been off the southeastern coast of North America. It was known as the Island of the Giant Turtles. The people used the bones of the giant turtles for tools, their meat for food, and their large shells to construct boats. The children were responsible for guarding the turtles' nests and eggs from predators, and ensuring that when they hatched, the young ones made it into the ocean. One time, the young people and the children were looking for a way to have fun. Even though they were told by their elders not to play with the turtles, when the parents were not looking, the children would ride the bigger ones. One group of kids got on top of a turtle that was moving into the deep water. The kids became stuck to the turtle. It looked like those children would be lost in the water, but then an old man showed up - he was an angel. He dipped his staff in the water, and it receded. The children were saved. This story teaches children to listen to their parents and not do things the wrong way.

On this Great Turtle Island, our ancestors began to realize that they were revolving around a great light. One day, they decided to go into a spiritual session with their medicine people to ask the Creator for a piece of that light. God responded by giving them the light they were asking for - they were given the light of the Eternal Flame, the Keetoowah sacred fire. With this gift, they were given strict instructions to watch over and take care of the fire. Today, the Keetoowah are known as the Keepers of the Fire. This story is sacred to our people. The elders realized that the earth they were living on was circling around a light, and, in communion with their Creator, a piece of that light was given to them. They celebrated this by gathering around the fire, singing to it, and holding it as sacred. Some anthropologists have written that the Cherokee worship the sun, but this is not true. They were given the fire to take care of it, maintain it, not abuse it, and to always send back a message of thanks through the fire's smoke. The Cherokee call this fire the Red Lady, or the Eternal Fire. It has been cared for by our people for generations, and the teachings of the Eternal Fire are passed down to our children. The fire is one of the four elements (air, water, and soil being the other three) that serves to connect that which is earth-bound with that which is not earth-bound. Together, they make up *elohi*, our world.

The fire at the Keetoowah stomp grounds in Oklahoma is 15,000 years old. That fire has been there since the 1700s and was cared for by our people. It originally came from the Keetoowah mounds in present-day North Carolina. Our time in this area, which we know as our Cherokee homelands, is what our ancestors referred to as the Third World, to which Keetoowah people migrated after their time on the Great Turtle Island. In our homelands, we developed many of the ceremonies and traditions that we know today, even though their form may have changed slightly over time. For example, in early documented history, such as the papers of John Howard Payne and Henry Timberlake, they record how, during that time, everyone in a Cherokee village did things together. The people always kept a fire in the middle of the village, and their settlements were always near a good running stream where they could approach from the west side and face the east with the water in front of them. The people awoke very early. Often, everyone was encouraged to wake up to observe the sunrise and to perform a morning ritual called "Going to Water." The men stood to the right, the women to the left, and the children in the middle. Some would totally submerge themselves and some would take off all their old clothes and have fresh clothes laid out at the bank to put on. Many of our traditions practiced today at the stomp grounds come directly from this ritual. They represent a continuation of how our early ancestors lived and began their day. In modern times, they perform the Going to Water ritual at least once or twice a year. They also enact the essence of this ritual through what they call "soup drink." In the summertime, we gather and break bread together to celebrate the good times we've had. In the olden times, this was called the "love feast." It represents the care we have for one another and how we are stingy with each other's existence, or as we say, *detsadageyusesdi.*

We are now living in what we observe as the Fourth World. Our Keetoowah ancestors left our homelands because there were so many conflicts, diseases, and other negative things emerging there. They left with promises by God that he would maintain order and peace if our people still held to his teachings. They would keep the fire he had given them. In each migration from the previous world, we are told that the Eternal Flame is to be foremost among our sacred holdings. The ones that left were labeled the Old Settlers, or the Western Cherokees. They came of their own volition and were already here when many of our people were removed by force along the infamous Trail of Tears. The Creator gave them the rule to strive to be the upmost human beings, and to treat each other and all other beings as equals; to value and respect all life. Even the name *Keetoowah* in our language strongly suggests that we not think less of anyone else. The word, *Gaduwagi,* which is another way to write *Keetoowah,* is how our people described themselves since the earliest times. In my opinion, it is also the oldest word in our language. The stories say that the Creator gave us this name. He told our ancestors that they will always be *Anigaduwagi* as long as they maintained and remembered the Original Teachings of love and spirit. These teachings are the key principles for how we must conduct ourselves as human beings. Our traditions as *Anigaduwagi* help us to never lose sight of that.

The single most important event for *Anigaduwagi* to remember these Original Teachings is an annual ceremony held during the "Moon of Need," *dulisdi.* This moon is between the months of September and October. This period is marked by the ending and the beginning of nature's growing cycle for all that is earth-bound. *Anigaduwagi* have always gathered to collectively acknowledge their interrelationship to all earthly things (*elohi gado nusdidanv*, or beings that are fixed to the earth) and heavenly entities (*galvlo daguwalosv*, or beings that exist above). This event observes the phenomenal earthly and heavenly collaboration that provides for the needs of the people. This period of time is also known as *atsila udetiyisgv,* the birthday of the sacred fire.

A fire (*atsila*) marks the center of this gathering place. This is called *atsila dihv* and it serves at the nucleus for all events, which include the communication link between heaven and earth. Therefore, it is observed as the most sacred place. During this annual ceremony, *Anigaduwagi* from all surrounding towns come to camp for several days and nights. This celebration is frequently called *digaduna'i* (town by town) or *sgadugi* (a term now used for the word "district"). There is fasting, rituals, "going to water," feasting, playful activities, recitations or preaching about renewal and the earth's life cycles, ceremonial dancing and singing, purification, prayer medicine, and other forms of communion.

While there were other seasonal and special celebrations held at the ceremonial grounds, when I was growing up, this celebration was the most significant. It was attended by Keetoowah people from all the other Cherokee towns, or communities. This celebration is perhaps the oldest continuous event in America. *Gaduwagi* elders have related that their grandfathers and grandmothers passed this annual ceremony down from generation to generation, as far back as can be remembered. *Dulisdi gaduna'i* occurs just as the occurrence of the four seasons: autumn, winter, spring and summer. The *Gaduwagi* sacred fire has been maintained and observed annually in this manner for thousands of years.

There have always been special Fire Keepers (*atsila anitiya*) whose responsibilities include the renewal of the fire. The fire must be renewed in a natural way - ignited from sparks of flint to naturally-derived substances, such as punk from the heart of various hardwood trees. No activities are to commence unless the Sacred Fire is burning. After the Fire Keepers are successful in starting the fire, they offer prayers to all people and are prepared to feed the Fire with the heart of various game animals. An offering of the "ancient one" (*tsola agayvli*, or tobacco) is also an option at this time. The seven Cherokee clans are included in the prayers and offerings. Once this is completed, the grounds are now ready for the people. The Fire Keepers must be in a constant state of readiness to do the task of maintaining the fire. They must not be affected by any ill or evil thoughts or have committed any wrongdoing; they must be renewed to cleanliness and purity through the taking of traditional medicine, fasting, and through performing the "going to water" ritual.

Prior to any ceremony to be held at the Sacred Fire, Medicine Workers (*nvwoti tsunilvwisdane*) gather to prepare the grounds, the time, and space. At the gathering, the Medicine Men collectively fast and use purification medicine. This gathering of the Medicine Workers is the most sacred mission performed by a collection of the most trusted *Gaduwagi* men. I am led to believe this Medicine Council (*dinilawiga*) began centuries ago. This core of men known only to the *Anigaduwagi* have always co-existed within our modern-day society. These sacred council missions can be as brief as a dawn to sun-up and "going to water" ritual, and as long as to four to seven days in advance of a ceremony to be held around the Sacred Fire. The Fire Keeper is usually an active participant in the medicine workers council. Frequently, the Fire Keeper builds an auxiliary Sacred Fire at the location of the gathering (*nvwa anodv*). The Medicine Council meetings are held at or near a designated leader's home or near the eastern perimeter of the clan arbors of the Sacred Fire. All aspects of life may be the focus of a Medicine Council.

After performing their spiritual tasks of meditation, fasting, "going to water," and preparing for the ceremony, the Medicine Workers are now spiritually correct and are issued an eagle feather to be worn in their hats throughout the ceremony as a symbol of worthiness to be *Gaduwagi* leaders. When I was young, I recall seeing these men move about the grounds visiting various family camps. The Medicine Workers were easily recognized - everyone knew them not only by their eagle feather, but by the shape and color of their hats, clothing, manner of walk and general appearance. Their presence seemed to have a calming impact on everyone. They were always a visible and constant reminder of the *Gaduwagi* way of life.

Some time ago, my brother Benny and I worked on this word, *Gaduwagi.* We thought about it together in a philosophical way, drawing from the teachings of our elders. It expresses our identity as a people: *Otsi Gaduwagi;* We are Keetoowah. It also expresses our core values. The meaning we arrived at was based on years of listening to our elders talking about the sacred fire. One of these elders was our father, Stokes Smith. He would say that the word describes *the image we are always supposed to follow and emulate* - the One Who Is Always Above. The name is a constant reminder to our people that there is a God up there, and that there isn't a person on the face of the earth who God does not know. The One Who is Above, *Wigaduwagi,* is always present. There, beyond the highest mountains that we can see, and from the greater mountain that is unseen, He cradles, embraces, and encircles all that is beyond, beneath, below, and in between. And supposedly the Original Messengers who represent the four original peoples live as high as possible - they stay at the highest possible points around our presence.

When someone is struggling, if you are a Keetoowah, you'll go over and help. You won't just sit there and watch. There emerges more of what we might call the Cherokee spirit. Thus, the term Keetoowah reflects *the image of all good things that people should reflect and strive for in life's journey.* It means that even if we must grovel around on Earth, we are still to follow this highest image that the word describes. The eagle feather reminds us of this image of something in high regard. Supposedly, Eagle can fly so high that he is near the Creator - in reality, that's just symbolism. Still, an eagle feather presented to an organization or to a person means they have gained so much honor, so much respect that, in a sense, they have gone over and above the call of duty. To be given one feather is enough to honor that.

According to the Original Teachings, living by the Creator's concepts of love and spirit while you walk on this earth earns you a place in the highest level of the afterlife, or heaven. In the traditional Keetoowah funeral, a person's body is carried around the fire seven times. The fire keepers light the fire on the day of the funeral and then let it burn for four days after. Anyone who requests a traditional funeral should be granted it. The Creator created seven levels of heaven. A person makes their record in life every day. This record is either wrong or right. The Creator judges by reviewing this record, and the person is placed on the according level of heaven. A person can move up if they act right and do good. The seventh level is the eternal level. This tells us that from a Keetoowah perspective, the body may die in this world, but the spirit remains in another dimension. It also tells us that there is no hell in our belief system. I remember a medicine man once said that people create their own hell through the choices they make in this life and in the afterlife. A living person can spiritually travel to the seventh, uppermost level of heaven if they intend to help save and protect life. The journey should not be attempted for personal gain or self-empowerment. It requires the use of love and the spirit that God gave you. You can only stay for what you came for, and then you must return back to the earthly world.

The Original Teachings often use the word *detsadageyusesdi.* When we say *detsadageyusesdi*, we are telling people to be stingy with one another in the way that a mother acts toward her child. To be stingy in this way is to love and hold tight to one another - to express that love by valuing everyone's unique contributions to the community. It is a way of being and thinking that honors and adheres to those ancient Original Teachings. So, our traditions and history offer a model for following these teachings. The acknowledgement of all-encompassing love is included in the Seven Original Bylaws given to us by the Creator. By never losing sight of the Creator's instructions, Keetoowahs are positioned to help all people re-learn them and put them into everyday use toward one another and all life. They are simple concepts, although they take hard work and dedication to apply to all that we say and do. And so, we understand that every Keetoowah custom is a reminder to renew your connection to the spirit world.

Chapter 2

The Importance of Women

Women have been blessed by the Creator with one of the strongest and purest gifts - the reproduction cycle. Cherokee women once had a very prestigious status in our culture. They were to be honored, protected, adhered to, and listened to - the highest stature of all. Somewhere down the line this was eroded and not preserved. This is where our people got off the beaten track, so to speak, in not honoring our women. In fact, they began to ostracize women from any activity who were on their monthly cycles. They had become fearful of that blood cycle. But really and truly that cycle is a very strong and pure medicine. Today, some of our medicine people have been taught to not have a female who is on her monthly cycle around them. I think they are fearful because they are not practicing a pure and true form of medicine.

Beyond our tribe, the Iroquois, of which the Cherokee and Keetoowah are distantly related, tell of the following legend. A two-headed monster came to a village and destroyed everything. It then went to the next village and began to destroy it, too. The people tried to kill the monster with all the weapons they had. They used their spears, axes, and clubs, but they could not subdue this evil force of destruction. The story goes that the monster was on its way to a Cherokee village. The people of the village wondered what they would do. The Seven Wise Men, representing each of the clans, went off to seek a vision. They went out separately and all came back with the same story. They were to find seven young women who had never been with men and were still pure and clean. It was to be when they were on their moon time or menstrual cycle. The older women of each clan were responsible for finding these young women who were in the first three or four days of their cycle. They were to dress them in pure white garments. Everything was to be pure and clean.

They instructed the women to wait at seven different stations, each strategically located along the path to the village in expectation of the monster's arrival. When the monster came to the first maiden, he was blinded by her power. He ducked his head and was really taken aback that she could stand there, strong and unaffected. He continued toward the village, and as he passed the second maiden, his movement became more difficult. After the third, he began to stagger. As he came to the fourth, he got sick and threw up a white bile, or life fluid. At the fifth one, he dropped to his knees and threw up yellow bile. He staggered again but arose and continued. Passing the sixth one, he became very ill and threw up black bile. As he approached the seventh one, he fell. He was crawling and vomiting red bile - blood. Then, he disintegrated. The seven young women had defeated the monster. Because of this feat, they became beloved clan mothers, and they taught their people about purity, cleanliness, and how to be in the world. The women were regarded so highly that they were given the big eagle feather, which is the highest honor one can receive. I remember when my dad told this story at the medicine council. He told it to remind everyone that women are to be highly regarded in our culture. It is not our way to mistreat or abuse women.

When the old ones talked about women, they always talked about strength - to the point where women were seen as the stronger of the sexes. Women demonstrated this strength in so many ways, and their emotions were a part of that. My father said that when a woman cries, she can still go on and have the strength to do what she needs to do. By contrast, when a man feels a certain way and yet tries to suppress his emotions, it is not a show of strength, but weakness. Women's emotions really show their strength in its purest form.

At the stomp grounds, the elders address the congregation with a spiritual lecture before certain events. This includes scheduled dances and annual celebrations, such as the state of the union or the commemoration of my grandfather Redbird Smith's birthday on July nineteenth. When they do this, each speaker stands before the ceremonial fire and relates their presence to the Red Lady of the Eternal Flame. For Keetoowahs, the Fire and the Spirit of the Woman God are inseparable. This Red Lady is able to take messages directly to the Creator. Although to my knowledge there is nothing mentioned about the role of a Woman God in all the literature, the Keetoowah always say, "She takes the message to the Original Father God," the Male God. The Woman God is the Mother to All, inseparable from the Red Lady of the Eternal Flame. And of course, there is the Child God, which is the Christ. In the early teachings, these are referred to as the Gods of All People.

First Woman: Selu, the Mother of Corn

In the beginning, Ye-Ho-Ha created Earth and all of the beings that live upon her. First Man and First Woman were sent to Earth to inhabit her. They were not mortal, but immortal beings, sent down by the Creator to caretake Mother Earth and to teach their two twin sons, who were mortal, how to live on the earth. Because the parents were not mortal, they did not have to work for their sustenance. Every few days when the family began to run out of food, mother would leave for the day and return in the afternoon with beans and corn. In the same way, when the family began to run out of meat, father would leave and return in a few days with a bountiful deer for provisions.

When the boys began to grow older, they became curious about the affairs of their parents. Soon they began to follow their mother, edging out a little farther each time they endeavored. By the time the boys were young men, they had accumulated enough courage to follow their mother completely. Of course, their mother was aware of her children's activities. Soon it was time for her to go and fetch the beans and corn that her family needed for survival. As she left, she knew that her sons would trail her again, and that this time they would follow her all the way. She asked them to stay and wait for their father to return and help him dress the deer. Instead, they waited for her to get down the path a ways, and then set out behind her.

They followed her to a place where a round, wooden building was standing. This circular home was different than their own, as the logs were standing in an erect circle. Their mother went inside of the structure and the boys peeked in between the logs to see what she was doing. When they looked in, they saw her singing and dancing around in a circle with her arms lifted up towards the sky. Soon, beans and corn began to pour out from underneath her arms and from her groin. Seeing this, the boys got scared and ran all the way home. They just knew that their mother was a sorceress, and they were going to have to kill her. Meanwhile, mother knew that the boys had seen her giving birth to their sustenance. She also knew that they were plotting her murder. But alas, she had foreseen that someday this could happen, and that there was nothing she could do about it but continue to love and provide for her children.

When their mother arrived home with the family's provisions, the boys approached her and told her what they had seen. The boys said that she was a sorceress, and that they would have to kill her. Their mother told the boys that she knew what they had done and their plan to murder her. She told them that this saddened her deeply, but that she still loved them very much and would always look down on them from heaven with favor, trying to help them in every way she could. She then told them that if they followed the instructions that she would give them, even though they murdered their own mother, they would not have to toil for their food. She told them that after they have killed her, they were to drag her body along the ground in rows. While they were doing this, they were to sing the songs and say the prayers that she would teach them, and dance in the way that she would instruct them. If they followed all of her instructions, corn would spring up and they would be fed. But if they didn't, they would have to toil and sweat to prompt the corn to grow.

The boys promised their mother that they would follow her instructions. They then killed their mother; however, they were disobedient to the instructions that she had given them. Instead, they rejoiced that they had killed a sorceress. When their father returned, he knew instantly what his children had done. He told them that they had done the wrong thing, that their mother was not a sorceress. He loved the boys and told them that their mother loved them so much that she would always watch over them from heaven. But the boys did not take much credence in what their father had said, because they felt that he was getting to be an old man and they were younger, stronger, and therefore, better.

In my interpretation of this ancient story, the First Woman had to be in the First World where people were still pure. In determining that their mother must be a witch, the boys forgot that she had always provided for them, ever since they had nursed off her breast and body. Their mother knew that they had decided to kill her. She told them that if they did what they planned, to destroy her, they would destroy the gift. Their food would have to be worked for and not given to them anymore. This is the Cherokee Corn Woman story. There is an inheritance of that gift, that women can produce the food for their families, take care of them and give them sustenance even when there is none. Women are also the standing support not only for the family but for men, too. Man has always brought hardship on himself.

Nancy Ward, the Last Cherokee War Chief

We know in our history and culture that Cherokee women can be warriors, not just men. In our early stories of the first coming of the white man, there was a woman who was known as Chief, or the Head of the whole Cherokee people. *Nanyehi,* or Nancy Ward, was the last recorded War Chief of the consolidated Cherokee Nation prior to removal on the Trail of Tears. Nancy's Cherokee name reflected her free spirit and her connection with the Little People, the *gunehi.* The legend goes that Nancy got the name as War Chief when she was fighting beside her first husband, Kingfisher. She was chewing his bullets to make them softer so that they shattered in the enemy. When he was mortally wounded, she picked up his gun and led the warriors to charge and smite their enemies.

Later on, Nancy married a white man named Bryant Ward, who was a Scots-Irish trader to the Indians. They had a daughter named Elizabeth "Betsy" Ward. Betsy went on to marry an immigrant from England named Brigadier General Joseph Martin and so became a prominent part of Euro-American history.

Nancy lived her life as a leader to her people. Through her leadership she set an example of compassion. According to one story, when she heard that some of her warriors were going against her and planned to attack a group of settlers, she herself swam across the river to warn the settlers of the impending attack. She saved them from certain death at the hand of the renegade warriors. This act endeared Nancy to the new colonizing government of the immigrants, but to her own people she was thought of as a traitor. Later, in her older years, she was once again revered by her people as a Beloved Woman. Nanyehi had influenced many peace treaties between her beloved Cherokee people and the colonizers, even as the new people continued to take over the land. Her last effort as an elder was to ensure peace for her people in their homelands. She tried to get her people to stay and not emigrate away from their lands, but she died before she could finish this goal. Not long after her death, the Trail of Tears ensued. Because of her courage and how she followed our traditional values to the end of her life, Nancy Ward is a Beloved Woman to all Cherokee people - including the eastern and western tribes.

There was once a rebellion among our people. It was called White Path's rebellion, around the late 1820s. White Path was an old chief; he was a highly respected traditional man. Around that time, there were many changes happening within our nation that affected Cherokee women and their role in our culture. Our new constitutional government valued men over women as elected leaders. With the endorsement of Cherokee women who had been opposing these changes, White Path led a peaceful rebellion that urged his people to remember the old ways that honored our women and the important forms of leadership they offered. In the end, the rebellion made some positive changes, but it wouldn't be until 1987 that our people would elect a woman as Principal Chief of the Cherokee Nation. That person was Wilma Mankiller (1945-2010), and she went on to serve two terms and earn a highly regarded status among her people and beyond.

Many women leaders from our Indian communities deserve recognition for their far-reaching and important contributions. Mary Golda Ross (1908-2008) was a Cherokee and became the first Native American aerospace engineer. Annie Dodge Wauneka (1910-1997) was a Navajo who served as a tribal council member for the Navajo Nation and worked in the public health field to reduce the incidence of tuberculosis in her community and across the country. Today, we see strong leadership modeled by American Indian women in the U.S. Congress, such as Deb Haaland (Laguna Pueblo) and Sharice Davids (Ho-Chunk). We should also honor the important work by Indian women attorneys, such as Melody McCoy (Cherokee) and Heather Kendall-Miller (Dena'ina Athabascan), both at the Native American Rights Fund. There are many others who contribute invaluably to their communities and the world.

Our reverence and respect for women should be held up as part of the sacred teachings of the Creator. We should never abandon this reverence and the status it affords women among our people. Our history shows us what happens when we stop valuing the contributions of our women and the sacred gifts they carry, we falter and lose sight of our traditional values. Our people become divided. We become easy to subdue by outside forces. We cease to model to others our sacred purpose in this world to live by the Original Teachings.

Chapter 3

Cherokee Games

Our traditional games, when played in the right way, promote physical, psychological, and spiritual well-being. They keep us healthy by encouraging us to be active and by bringing people together for enjoyment in a community setting. Competition used to be very intense in some games, but today Keetoowah people view them as activities to inspire and teach ideal behaviors and positive character traits. For example, the stickball game experienced this transformation from a highly competitive and violent activity in earlier times to an event that is now practiced at our ceremonial grounds and is intended only for good-natured play within the community. In this way, many of our ceremonial activities revolve around the game because of what it represents to the Keetoowah people. There are also "smaller games" that I will describe - some of which have fallen out of play and others that Cherokees still play regularly today. While these smaller games don't carry the same ceremonial significance as stickball, they make for a good pastime when Cherokee people get together.

The Stickball Game

The original stickball game was very brutal. Many people died or were maimed during these games. Cherokee warriors played against other tribes, or even other Cherokee villages, to settle disputes. People used bad medicine and conjuring to affect players' performance and to otherwise sway the outcome of the war-like game, which was also the object of intense gambling. In fact, the game was often called *dahnuwa usdi* - "little war." There is an old story about a strip of land between the Creeks and the Cherokees somewhere around the border of what we know as Georgia and Alabama. The east side was claimed by the Cherokees and the Creeks claimed the west side. The head chiefs of each tribe decided to hold a ball game to see who would be able to claim the strip of land in between. The Creeks came from the west, chanting and whooping, and the Cherokees arrived from the east. The game started at sunrise. Many warriors were killed in that game, but by sundown, the Cherokees defeated the Creeks and claimed that strip of "no man's land." Not too long ago, a major highway was being planned over this area. The surveyors and construction crew found the burial grounds of each side's warriors.

Today, the Keetoowah stickball game does not follow this original form that was once the realm of warriors. Instead, it includes everyone in the community. It is played outdoors and near the sacred fire, and, in this way, it teaches how to live in harmony with the elements of nature and reminds us that there is a Supreme Being, a Great Provider. It is played in the spirit of congenial admiration, which encourages positive individual, group, and community interactions. It is also played to honor and respect the autonomy and worth of every individual, a belief that each and every one contributes to the well-being of the community. Players must be responsible for one another's safety and not jealous of anyone's success. In this way, it is played in accordance with Keetoowah cultural values that promote honesty and integrity. The group play honors the opinion of each person equally; decisions are arrived at by consensus. Overall, the game helps to increase one's knowledge of the total nature of the community and Keetoowah lifeways - that we may all be individuals, but in the community, and in God the Creator, we find strength.

The stickball playing area is approximately one hundred feet square. A pole, a complete tree trunk approximately forty feet tall, stands at the very center. The pole is marked around the perimeter at about fifteen feet from the top, and a wooden carving of a fish approximately twenty inches long, eight inches tall, and three inches thick, is placed at the top of the pole.

Some poles have a wooden ball about the size of a basketball at the top. A small ball, just a little bigger than a golf ball, is used for play. It is a firm ball, made of tightly packed animal fur and covered in soft leather. The ball sticks are about thirty inches long and made of Hickory. They form an open cuff laced with leather to catch hold and throw the ball. Sticks are used in pairs by the men only.

The object of the play is to hit the wooden fish or ball at the top of the pole. While men must use ball sticks, women players need to only use their hands to handle the ball. This affords the women a natural advantage and equalizes physical strengths and abilities. When women are in possession of the ball, men can tease, distract, or make motions to hinder or delay her throw - for example, you'll hear them say *hiyosdasi!* which means "interfere!" or "distract!" After a period of time, she must be allowed to throw the ball. When a woman has a ball and is looking to gain a favorable position to throw it, the other women on the team can interfere and hold the men back, or even grab their ball sticks. If this happens, the man must hold still until his ball sticks are released. While in the grasp of a woman, men pretend that they are trying hard to escape. This is intended to add humor and fun. However, the women can vigorously push, pull, and otherwise be rough with the men, but men must be careful not to let go of their ball sticks. Furthermore, women can take the ball out of a man's sticks or cause the ball to be dropped. Men are never to resort to using their hands by catching or holding the ball. If a man is at risk of losing the ball, the other men start yelling *tsaligo!* or "you have partners!", which signals him to pass the ball. If the ball goes out of bounds, then the players yell, *ayehli!* (center). The ball must then be tossed back to the center of the playing area and all players have an opportunity to catch it.

Just prior to the beginning of the play, all players are instructed to not get angry and to be careful with each other. The play begins when the ball is thrown with the ball stick as high as possible. The players yell or whoop loud and enthusiastically each time the ball is raised for the start of the play. As the ball comes down it may be caught before it hits the ground by any player. If the ball is caught, it is thrown at the wooden fish. If the ball is not caught and hits the ground, an all-out scramble ensues until a player can pick it up and throw it at the target at the top of the pole.

This is repeated each time a player attempts to score by throwing the ball upward toward the pole. Players score seven points by hitting the fish at the top of the pole. One point is given if the ball hits the pole above the mark. When a player scores, this starts a new play with a fresh ball, which symbolizes a renewal or fresh start - just like in life when one accomplishes a meaningful goal.

The score is kept using tally marks on the ground on either side of a line from the pole to the sacred fire. One side represents the women, and the other side is for the men. The markings are about two feet in width and a half foot apart. Each side is responsible for keeping their own scores. When the tally marks reach the fire mound, then they reverse back to reach to the pole again. The first side to reach back to the pole wins the game. At any given time, the players can be grandpa, dad, uncle, brother, son, cousin, brother-in-law, versus grandma, mother, sister, aunt, daughter, and so on. Players may enter or leave the game at any time. There is not an official number of players required to play and there is no referee. Disagreements and arguments are nonexistent. Instead, words of enjoyment and encouragement abound.

This way of playing stickball is a result of decisions that our ceremonial leaders made in the past to account for dire circumstances. Due to increased external pressures of assimilation around the turn of the twentieth century that threatened to terminate their beloved way of life, Keetoowah elders and the Keetoowah medicine council convened in the old way to formulate strategies and actions that would save, sustain, promote and perpetuate Keetoowah precepts. They arrived at a consensus that the stickball game would be one of these continuation strategies and would reinforce community values and resist the termination of the Keetoowah people. In essence, the elders took the original, war-like stickball game and renewed it to the present-day community play. Since this time, the Keetoowah stickball game has served as an unwritten grand design purpose to promote, develop, strengthen, and instill community values. It provides the guidelines for living well and in a righteous way. One such guideline deals with the need to periodically begin various aspects of life anew. In fact, the green stripe you see on the ball sticks represent the renewal of values in the community.

The Cherokee word for the ceremonial stomp grounds is *gatiyo*. This word is derived from *nigatiyo*, which means "all together." The sense of community at the stomp grounds is experienced through a spirit of belonging, a feeling of kinship, and positive interpersonal relationships and solidarity. In playing stickball, there are countless opportunities for the members of the community - young and old - to demonstrate community values. The game brings great enjoyment to the players and onlookers. This could be construed by outsiders as simply entertainment, however, stickball serves as a vital part of our ceremonies. It is an important rule at the stomp grounds to hold a stickball game before and after each night of ceremonial dancing around the fire. Weather permitting, stickball has been played by the Keetoowah people in this way practically every week for over a hundred years. When you look at it this way, stickball is inseparable from our communal worship both because of what it symbolizes and how our ceremonies are organized around its play.

On the fourth Saturday of each month, Keetoowah people hold ceremonial dances around the sacred fire to express appreciation for the Creator's blessings. Meetings are also held every Sunday, and these are called ball playing days. All men, women, and children participate in a congenial, joyful game of Cherokee ball. After six of these Sunday meetings, the Keetoowahs prepare for what is called a "soup drinking," or "love feast." In preparing for the feast, everyone hunts and fishes throughout the previous week to provide meat for the soup. Although the soup is the main course, many other dishes accompany this meal.

On the Saturday before the seventh ball game, an all-night ceremonial dance is held. On Sunday, after the ceremonial chiefs have done their preaching and the seventh ballgame has been played, the soup drink feast begins. But before anyone begins to eat, each person puts a small portion of the soup on the ground. This signifies giving back to Mother Earth a small portion of what has been taken. The "love feast" is a time when the people gather to cherish each other and the events of the past games. Winning or losing is not given much importance, except for the lighthearted teasing to remind the losers that they have to serve the winners the soup drink.

In the weeks it takes to play stickball seven times, the players have learned about others and have demonstrated their own integrity in the process. The Keetoowahs celebrate this sense of community and interdependence at the end with a ceremonial dance and a feast. To me, this has no equal in promoting an appreciation for a strong sense of community. I believe Native American cultural values are grounded in the innate power of caring - a sense of community. Each of us with Cherokee blood carries this innate sense. The stickball game that our Keetoowah elders and medicine council designed recognizes this sense of community and we play the game in solidarity and unity with all life. The elders were fully aware that in playing this game, people could best demonstrate their care for each other. Stickball displays the responsibility that each member of the Keetoowah community has for the collective. Yes, there is competition, but that is carried out with clear appreciation for each person's contribution to the whole. You can feel this when you are near a Keetoowah community. You will hear the laughter and whooping of joy, and this is synonymous with our cultural survival and strength as a people.

Smaller Games

The Marble Game

On their days off, our people would gather together and play a number of marble games. People used to make their own marbles from stone that was chipped and rounded. These marbles were very close in size to modern-day billiard balls, and today people mostly use these for play, with the cue ball being favored. Some say that the origin of the marble game began with the Devil challenging the Son of Man to a similar type of game. The reward to the winner was control over all humankind. They began the game at sunrise, and around sundown, the Son of Man defeated the Devil. This ensured that humans would have control over themselves.

There are many varieties of marble games, but the one that our people still play today requires an outdoor field with four divots dug out in the ground, about four to five paces apart in a straight line. The last divot has another one a few paces just to the right of it, making a total of five "holes" in the ground. The holes are approximately two inches in diameter and a player must rest their marble exactly atop the hole to advance to the next one. Any number of players can join in the game. Throughout the game, players attempt to roll their marble on top of the nearest hole, while also attempting to hit their opponents' marbles out of the way. Often, the game is played tournament-style, with two to three players per team. These tournaments can be very lively to watch, as the players employ great strategy and skill.

There are other varieties of marble games, however, they have fallen out of play these days. One uses a square field with marbles set up in holes located in each corner and one in the middle. Each player would be on one side about twelve or fifteen paces away and their partner would be on the other side. The object was for each team to get as many marbles as they could out of the holes. The number of marbles set up on the field was decided by the players and would determine what it took to win. These games would often incite people to gamble and fight, and some would put all that they own on the line. Inevitably, some people would lose, and they often became suicidal as a result. The traditional Keetoowah did not endorse that kind of game. Their game was more aligned with the friendship game that honored the Son of Man giving self-control to all people.

Yet another marble-type game would involve picking out a large stone. The people would try to throw that stone as far as they could, and who ever could throw it the furthest would win. They called this game "chuggin'," and again, Cherokees would often use this game to wager money and gamble. Players would pay to be in the game, and whoever won would take the money pot. The traditional Keetoowah does not honor this game, either.

Chunkey

Chunkey is one of the oldest games recorded in prehistory. It was played by many different southeastern native tribes. It originates from the ancient city of Cahokia. Chunkey spears were eight- to ten-feet long and made out of Hickory or Poplar wood. The chunkey stones, or discs, were made of either sandstone or granite. Stone sizes would vary from six inches in diameter with a concave or convex side and about two inches thick. Some stones had holes in the middle of them for versions in which the spears were thrown through the openings. More commonly, the spears were thrown at the estimated place where the chunkey stones would "fall." The players would throw their spears as the chunkey stone was rolled down a flat clay-packed court with a fine sandy layer on top. This field was about one hundred feet long and twelve feet wide. The players would often run parallel to their sticks as if to encourage the flight. Whichever spear landed closest to the chunkey stone when it stopped rolling received the point.

Each community or tribe had variations on the sizes of the stones and spears and court parameters, but essentially the game was played in the same way. Traditionally, this game was taken very seriously and was also a gambling game. Chunkey games were played for hours, sometimes days. Spectators filled the chunkey yard, and some accounts of this game describe a frenzied atmosphere fueled by excitement and betting. Like certain marble games, sometimes people would gamble away all of their possessions and would become suicidal as a result. The chunkey stones themselves would be part of the winnings. Many ancient burial mounds contain chunkey stones that have been buried next the individual in death. The game seemed to die out after the early colonial period, although no one knows why this is so. Today, chunkey is not a commonly played game.

The Cornstalk Shooting Game

Long ago, Cherokee hunters and warriors developed a game in which they could test their accuracy with the bow and arrow. After the harvest, they would gather the cornstalks in the fields, stack them together horizontally, and compete to see who could pierce the most cornstalks with their arrows. Cherokee people still play this game today, and it hasn't changed much. The cornstalks are stacked one foot deep and three feet high. They are held between hickory sticks that are sunk into the ground and tied together at the top. Each player walks one hundred yards away and stands facing the target. For each round, the players are allowed to shoot two arrows. The score is tallied by the number of stalks that the arrow tips penetrate. The first player to reach fifty points is the winner.

Only traditional, hand-made bows are allowed in the game. These bows are made from various woods, such as Hickory, Black Locust, or the preferred Bois d'Arc (Osage Orange) wood, which possesses an ideal combination of strength and flexibility. The arrows that players use for the cornstalk shoot have metal shafts instead of arrowheads. There is no limit on the length of these shafts, but they are usually five to eight inches long.

In recent history, players would pay a fee to get into the game. The grand prize would typically be a butchered hog quartered into various parts, along with the entry fees of all the participants. So, the more players in the game, the more money the winner would take. Again, according to traditional Keetoowah values, gambling or making money on this game is not approved. The game is supposed to be for enjoyment and fellowship.

These smaller games provided a fun pastime for Cherokees to play or spectate during their days off, but our traditional Keetoowah people did not endorse the gambling and other harmful behaviors that sometimes accompanied them. Instead, the traditional Keetoowah stickball game upholds community values and results in positive feelings among all who play. Because of this, and because it is played near the sacred fire, we consider it a sacred sport.

Chapter 4

Messengers

The world is full of messengers. If you really stop to listen to them, you can understand what the Creator is trying to tell you. God comes to us in strange ways. Sometimes this is through animals that are behaving abnormally. For example, a young man once came to me for help with interpreting such a message. He told me that a roadrunner had hopped on the hood of his moving vehicle and began to peck at the windshield. At that point, I had to take stock of what this encounter with the road runner meant. In these situations, I use a pendulum to ask God to tell me the meaning of the message. My inquiry revealed that someone was watching that person. I then followed up in my reading to check if law enforcement was involved. My inquiry came back affirmative. This meant that the person was involved in something illegal and the law had him under surveillance. At this point, I said if he tells me the truth and comes clean, then I can help him. If he does not, then he cannot be helped. Roadrunner came to give a message to that boy.

Eagle, especially the Bald Eagle, is a carrier of good messages. Even just seeing an eagle is a good omen. Eagle is one of the creations that God chose to guard His home. Hawk, Redtail Hawk especially, also carries a good message. Horned Owl and Screech Owl bring mostly negative messages, but you have to look into the encounter. You have to check each member of your family to see if the owl is trying to tell you that someone is sick. Reptiles - especially those coming into your home or personal area - always connote something evil. Coyote and Wolf are carriers of bad messages, but this is all according to how they come across you. If the coyote or wolf acts peculiar and stares at you, it is telling you that something is wrong. If a wolf crosses the road in front of you from right to left, watch out and be careful how you drive or walk on that path or road. But if a wolf crosses you from left to right, it's actually a good message. Fox is the carrier of bad gossip. Messages from God can come to you in any of these creatures. In some cases, God allows a deceased person's spirit to appear to you. This may be to warn you of oncoming injury or sickness. In other cases, it might be a good omen.

The Red Lady of the Eternal Flame is also a messenger. She is the Mother God, and she carries your prayers back to the Father God and the Child God. Your prayers will get through if you do this in a good way and with a good mind. In the human realm, there are four major Prophet Messengers that relate to four major medicine plants. These are the Red, Blue, Black, and Yellow clan messengers. The Red or Brown Clan, known as the Earth Guardians and who are endowed with great spirituality, correlates with a shrub plant commonly known as Red Root. The Blue Clan, known as the Universal Ones and who are endowed with exploration qualities, correlates with the Cedar Tree - particularly one that has been struck by lightning and survived. The Black Clan, known as the Old Ones and who are endowed with great physical strength, correlates with the plant commonly called Ginseng. The Yellow Clan, known as the Wise Ones and who are endowed with intuition, correlates with the plant commonly called Goldenseal. These plants will be further explained in the next chapter. It should be noted that in the practice of traditional medicine, these four plants are considered the most powerful of all. A practitioner's medicine usually contains at least one of these four plants that correlate with the Prophet Messengers.

Messages can also come to us during our sacred rituals. In the Sacred Water Ritual, I must make a circle in the middle of the water. I offer a prayer so that the Creator can give me instruction. If activity or objects appear inside the circle I have made, it means that somebody may be inflicting injury or disease on another person. I have to read up on it with my pendulum and try to find out what it means. In one of my practices of a water reading of this sort, a large black leach came into the circle.

You see, the circle signifies the world, and in this case, it signifies the world of the person for whom I am performing the ritual. The leach had to be expelled. I used a stick to spear the leach and a cry came out of it, a human sounding cry. The people who were getting the treatment heard that crying. That meant another person had directed negativity toward the people getting the treatment.

Of course, God can also deliver messages to you directly. One time I was doing a spiritual reading at the edge of a stream. For this kind of reading, you must stay still and commune with the water. I could hear footsteps coming toward me. The footsteps kept getting closer and closer. They came so close that I opened my eyes to see what it could be. But by opening my eyes, I broke the spell - I could see nothing there. I thought, if I would have stayed still, He would have put his hand on me. I turned around, and across the circle a willow bush shook without any wind. That was God. He was still there. This demonstrates that sometimes the Creator can use plants to visit you. As in this story, sometimes when there is no wind at all you might see a limb shaking or you might hear a tree fall in the forest but not see it. Each time you have to check it out and see if it is a message from God.

Very few people have come face-to-face with God. This has happened to me - it was a supreme experience in my life. It occurred during a time when I was depressed and in conflict. I wanted to give up on practicing medicine. I was walking in a familiar place, near a canyon of sorts that has a chimney rock formation. I don't know when I fell or when I came to, but I found myself on my back, unable to move. It occurred to me that I might be dead. I wasn't dead, but I was still in denial and deep despair - so much that I wanted to be dead. I thought that death could be my way out of the problem I was experiencing in my life. Just then, out of the corner of my eye, I saw myself standing in the air. I saw my spirit on top of the chimney rock. My body was still on its back, and I could see myself - my spirit - trying to get down from there. Then a small light came out of the deep, dark canyon. I knew what that was, but I was still in denial. The closer it came, the bigger the light got, but in my denial, I still did not want to confirm what that light was.

When the big white light came within fifteen feet of that chimney rock, it illuminated everything. In that light appeared God. He held out His hand and let my spirit come down from the chimney rock. He brought me down and showed me a lot of things, including people that had gone before me. In this episode, God lifted my depression and denial. I got my mind back and my pride. He brought me the original teachings to all people and brought me new medicine to use. He renewed my love and my sacred spirit. My spirit traveled through the wind, which is the connector to everything. He taught me only to seek assistance from Him and nothing else. Four days later, that God who appeared to me as a light again appeared on the door to my medicine room - this time in the form of the Mother God, the Father God and the Child God. Therefore, they are the biggest messengers I know.

I have described this encounter before in my first book, *Stand as One*, where you can also see a picture of that door. I tell the story again here because it completely changed my life. Another phenomenal moment in my life occurred when I was asked to help with the release of rehabilitated Bald Eagles near the Sequoyah Wildlife Refuge. Victor Roubidoux, who manages the Iowa Tribe's Grey Snow Eagle House, asked me to provide a blessing for this event. After the birds were released, they flew circles over my head. This moment was captured in the photo you see with me and others who witnessed this event. I'm pictured with my young granddaughter, Kellie Marie Smith, to the right, and her father, Crosslin Smith, Jr. holding a camera in the bottom right.

The early teachings of the Mother God, the Father God, and the Child God are for all peoples. These teachings instruct us to acknowledge in our prayers *all* people - of yesterday, today, and tomorrow. Acknowledging those of yesterday pertains to the ones who have already lived and died. We believe that there is no eternal death. It's only a change-over from this Earth to where we go in spirit. The Spirit is an external extension of existence. As I described before, there is no hell. Rather, there are seven levels of heaven. If one does not first go to the seventh, or highest, level, then you will inhabit one of the lower levels. In the lower levels, people can try again to live well. If they do what they are supposed to do, they will ascend to a higher dimension.

There is a story of the Great Speckled Bird that took some Keetoowah

Another phenomenal moment in my life. Unknown photographer

people to heaven. The flight was so fast it almost blinded the people he was carrying. They visited God and his angels, and when they were ready for the Great Speckled Bird return them to Earth, the head angel wanted to keep one of the Earth people. This woman was pregnant, and he wanted to keep her child. But God would not allow this. There was a conflict between God and the head angel, so God threw him down to Earth. This angel became the devil, or Lucifer, according to the Bible. When the Great Speckled Bird brought the Earth people back, the fallen angel was there waiting for them. He wanted to consume the baby. God sent the pregnant woman a pair of eagle wings and instructed her to fly into the forest to where a large serpent lived. God further instructed her to eat from the mouth of the serpent. He told her that this would protect her and her baby. From that story, our traditional people learned to bless water with the snake song, and to ask pregnant women to drink it so that their baby will be delivered easily into the world.

The Keetoowahs honor all peoples living today. They also honor all people on their way to be born into this world. In their ancient prayer, when done in the right way, they honor and become one with the unborn Christ before He came into this world. The greatest honor of my life is to share with you the most ancient gift from the Creator - the way He taught us to pray. To be in communion with our God, we are to silence everything that we have. Silence your eyes and look inside yourself. Silence your ears; hear nothing but the inner voice. Be one with the special gift that the Creator gave you - your spirit that is a piece of His spirit. Know the child with which He began your life - your energy, your curiosity, your innocence. Honor and respect all peoples of the earth; honor and respect all living things. In doing so, you also show honor and respect for yourself.

These prayers will help you invest in this duty to carry on our ancient Native American traditions. These concepts were born out of the dream of the Cherokee people, wherever their spirits may be. To become a recipient of Spirit removes us from our physical bodies. We are required to be one with everything for a moment. Once this is accomplished, there are unlimited resources, forces, and energies available to you. We consider the four elements that are extended to every life form as sacred. First is the Air. We confirm the fact that we are all connected to everything by air. Next, the Water. We confirm that we are connected to everything by water. Then, the Heat, or Fire. We confirm that we are connected to everything by heat, especially the Eternal Flame. Lastly, we confirm that we are connected to all life by the planet Earth - the Soil. When those confirmations have been accomplished, you walk on a clear and pure path that leads to a successful and enjoyable life.

The Creator entrusted our ancestors with another form of communion as a teaching that should be shared with all people. It is as follows: At this moment in time, for all times, we deliver our names and our clans to the Creator. Then we ask the Creator for a divine intervention against all negative things. We use this gift the Creator gave us when we were born. He gave us love and His spirit. Those two elements have always been in our body. We ask the Creator to renew these two elements, and we ask Him to help us to become one with love and spirit, body and soul. When we do this in the right state of mind, we become one with the loving spirit of God.

This prayer then can be delivered to the Red Lady of the Eternal Flame so that she can give it as a messenger to the Father God and the Child God. This is a reunification of the loving spirit we have, the loving spirit He gave us. He is the one that will give us a divine blessing, a divine cleansing, that will result in success in everything we want to do. Because we so appreciate these elements that are extended to us, we offer our own traditional thanksgiving song in return. The sounds of the song could never be understood by anyone but God. However, we believe that the sounds are universal. The song goes in this manner:

O-hi-na-a-du

O-hi-na-a-du

O-hi-na-a-du

O-hi-na-a-du

A-du may mean the name of God in the Latin language.

The next part is:

Wi-hi-na-ha-du

Wi-hi-na-ha-du

Wi-hi-na-ha-du

Wi-hi-na-ha-du

And then:

Wi-hi-yo

Wi-hi-ya

Ya-wi-hi-ye

Wi-hi-ya

This last part repeats all the way through two times. This thanksgiving song is to say: "And we have come before God, and before God, we ask Him to not let us fail or perish at the hands of negativity. From the beginning of their lives, you have given them love and spirit."

Chapter 5

Plant Medicines

The Creator provided all the plants that we use for healing. In the practice of traditional medicine, plants are helpers. They can help heal people, but only through a spiritual communion with the Creator. In my work, I have found that our traditional Indian medicine can be more effective than that of Western doctors. One example is a common plant we call Broomweed. One of my clients came to me with an advanced case of diabetes in addition to prostate cancer. The cancer had spread through his bones, and his foot was black up to his knee. His doctor wanted to amputate most of his leg to address the blackness caused by nerve damage, but the man refused and came to see me about the issue. After performing a spiritual reading, I gave him a gallon of Broomweed and told him how to take it. After he took the first gallon, the blackness cleared up in his foot. At that time, I gave him a second gallon of the medicine. When he finished this second dose, the infection in his leg and foot was clear. My client went back to his doctor and showed him his leg and foot without any infection. The doctor assessed that his heartbeat had normalized. He was shocked. He wanted to know what the man had done. Well, the man told his doctor that he had quit the doctor's medicine and started using Indian medicine. The doctor was in disbelief and asked what was in the medicine I gave him. They always want to know what we use, even if their medicine doesn't believe in our methods.

I learned about Broomweed from my uncle. He told me that my grandmother (his mother) used to make a tea out of it when the kids got sick. With this knowledge, my uncle performed a spiritual reading to see if it would work against a whooping cough epidemic that had afflicted our community. He got an affirmative reading. He told me he gathered a bunch of Broomweed and boiled it in a large pot. When it cooled, he used a gourd dipper and had the people line up to drink that tea out of the dipper. Sure enough, it helped them. In my own research and readings, I checked to see if that plant could be used to subdue COVID-19, the coronavirus pandemic. I got an affirmative reading. The affirmation said that it could prevent people from catching the virus. If they did catch it, the medicine could lessen the symptoms and help them get through the sickness. So far, in my practice, we have had a high success rate with this treatment.

Although Broomweed is common, it is a very special plant that our people have used for generations. It also helps to relieve depression from any part of the body. Boneset is another plant we used in the same way as Broomweed. During the Spanish flu pandemic of 1918, my uncle told me he used Boneset tea to treat it. You can combine Boneset and Broomweed to make a more powerful healing tea. You have to keep the Boneset cool so it won't spoil, but you can keep the Broomweed out at room temperature for a certain length of time.

Traditional healers view medicine as the act of healing someone's spirit that has been wounded. In many cases, a wounded spirit leads to other dysfunctions of the body. The cause of the original wound could be something foreign that enters the body and upsets the natural balance. This results in sickness, and although two individuals may exhibit similar symptoms, traditional healers know that the root cause of that sickness may actually be different. This is the main difference between Western medicine and what we call Indian medicine. Indian medicine is used to regain balance. When something is in disarray or out of esteem, someone who is elderly and wise about the use of medicine helps get the person back in harmony or balance.

Many healers who are wise in this way know that everything has a frequency. Our bodies have a vibration. Those who are skilled in the ways of

Indian medicine can become very sensitized to the frequencies or vibes that people's bodies emit. They can then read the frequencies, which informs them on how to treat the individual. Some would call this "energy healing" - the act of suppressing energy or causing the energy in someone to rise. Regardless, no Indian medicine is ever done without a spiritual consultation or focusing one's mind in a spiritual way. As a boy, and later as a young man, I watched my father do readings. While he was performing these readings, he would sit motionless - almost like he was in hypnosis. While he was in this trance mode of reaching the situation, evidently, he was fulfilling the spiritual requirements of Indian medicine. With that acknowledgement and involvement of the spirits, he could determine some course of action to treat a patient - what to use, what not to use, where he would get it, what directions would it come from, and so on. All these things would be considered in a comprehensive manner.

There are stark differences between Western and Indian ways of healing. Unfortunately, many of our Indian ways have been ridiculed or looked down upon, when in fact they have a lot to offer. People might view some of our traditional healing practices as unsanitary, for example, the act of blowing air or spewing water on a patient as one method they used. But in all my young life, I do not remember ever going to a Western doctor. Our father did all the medicine work. He would doctor us for belly aches and headaches and could treat wounds or cuts - he knew how to do these things and we lived well. The first Western doctor I visited was a dentist.

You may be wondering what it takes to be a traditional doctor. There is a spiritual discipline that it requires. I would say that many people could pursue this if they would - and yet, the *would* part eliminates a lot of people. The same elements are available for everyone to draw upon, but not everyone has the discipline it takes to make oneself divine, to make oneself worthy. Making oneself completely worthy to do the work of "the One Up Above" is not something that everyone is willing to do. The One Up Above is, of course, the Creator - the one who provides everything. In Cherokee, we really don't mean "Creator." The word in our language, *Unehlvnvhi*, more accurately means "the Provider." We're talking about the Divine Being or Presence up there who provides us with everything. How that provision is made is a collaboration of what we call "Our Father up there," and "Our Mother here on Earth." Nothing is provided unless those two collaborate. When they collaborate, the things that we can use are provided and produced for us.

To make oneself completely worthy to do this work has to be enacted, not simply professed. The ancestors, the old ones, through their actions and activities, ritualistically placed themselves in a position that earned them a worthiness to do "His work." If you only profess it, you've said you are something before you've shown that you can actually do it. To say, "I commit myself to this," is not enough. You have to live it. Fasting is one way. You fast to deprive the of body of comfort so that you may achieve a heightened spiritual awareness, or a vision. Your thoughts are a lot more sensitive and they become keener when you prepare yourself in this way. This is what the old ones, the medicine men, would do when they came together to make medicine for the community. It's what our spiritual people have done since time immemorial. In today's world, we see many who profess to be healers. There are those who say they have a healing touch and can cure people by laying their hands upon them. I would not say that I disbelieve them, but unless I know that someone has actually deprived themselves of life's pleasures to reach a point where they can work with someone who needs their help, I don't know what kind of confidence I'd have in them.

Medicine and plants should never be used in a negative manner. To try and manipulate people or the things they want by means of taking away goods from another person is taboo in a traditional culture. There's a Cherokee word that describes how "something came in and mixed in with their medicine." In my interpretation, this concept of bad medicine had to come from the outside. It's not a part of our traditional teachings about healing and medicine. Some anthropologists think that witchcraft already existed in many of the Native American tribes, but I think that witchcraft was introduced by the Europeans. We can see this in how they burned people at the stakes in old England. I think Indian bad medicine is influenced by the witchcraft of that part of the world. Those who practice bad medicine think they can take something that belongs to you, something that you habitually use, or a piece of your hair or some fingernail clippings, to cause you harm from a distance. That means they can be physically in one town but can be conjuring someone in another town. This is a big, big taboo in our traditional culture.

At the stomp grounds, they try to keep the making of medicine as pure as can be. As a young man, I watched our medicine men at the ceremonial grounds arrive a day or so early - maybe four days - before a meeting would take place. They would do all kinds of things to purify themselves, and they did a lot of thinking before they ever talked to one another. They would come together to offer their spiritual readings, and then they would disperse. One would take off down toward the cliff, one toward the watering hole - all different places. They'd be given an amount of time just to go and meditate, sort of like seeking a vision to find out things. Then they would reconvene and talk about these things, about the spiritual dimension they had observed and what it might mean for the community.

Traditional tobacco is one of our oldest medicines that we still use to treat many illnesses today. It is one of our most sacred plants given to us by the Creator. In truth, nothing can be done to make this plant better than it is in nature, as God has created it. The plant is different from the commercial variety that is used in tobacco products. We call it "old tobacco" - *tsoli agayvli,* and in addition to its use as a medicine, we use it to give an offering when we pray. It is a sacred plant that we offer back to the Creator in thanks for the blessings He has given us. The Creator did not intend for this plant to be smoked. The purest way to use it in prayer is just as it is, although we often dry it after it has finished its growing cycle. One of the strongest prayers we can make involves this plant and acknowledges all of creation. Take a small amount of the plant and offer it to the Brown people of yesterday, today, tomorrow, and for all time. Take another small amount and offer it to the Blue people of yesterday, today, tomorrow, and for all time. Offer some to the Yellow people of yesterday, today, tomorrow, and for all time. Then offer some to the Black people of yesterday, today, tomorrow, and for all time. Next, offer some to the earth upon which every living thing depends. Offer some to the heavens - the sky and cosmos. In this, your prayer covers all life beyond earth, if it exists. Lastly, offer some to the spirit that the Creator gave you when you were born. In this, you reunify your spirit with the Creator's spirit.

Traditional tobacco is one of the seven most powerful and sacred medicine plants. Included in the representations of the first four are the Original Prophet Messengers mentioned in the previous chapter. Together, they make the strongest purifying medicine that is representative of seven holy beings, what some might call angels. The tea that these sacred plants make when combined in water is our Holy Water, or what we call the Blood of the Earth.

ᎣᏓᎵ ᎦᎸ / Odali Galv / Ginseng: Representing the Black Prophet Messenger, this plant is an all-around medicine that can be used for any ailment and enhances the healing properties of anything it is combined with.

ᏳᏈᎳ / Yugwila / Goldenseal: Representing the Yellow Prophet Messenger, this plant is used as a helper to acquire the necessary needs such as food, clothing, household goods, and money. Many of our mothers, who are the heads of households, used to have a small red cloth sack with Goldenseal inside and carried it in their purses so that they would always have the necessary needs for their families.

ᏗᎵᎦᎵᏍᎩ ᎤᏍᏗ / Diligalisgi Usdi / Red Root: Representing the Red or Brown Prophet Messenger, this plant is used for the purification of the body.

ᎠᏥᎾ ᏧᏍᏓᏲᎯᏍᏗ / Atsina Tsusdayohisdi / Lightning Struck Red Cedar: Representing the Blue Prophet Messenger, this plant is used to create a serene environment.

ᏦᎵ ᎠᎦᏴᎵ / Tsoli Agayvli / Ancient Old Tobacco: Representing all peoples of yesterday, today, tomorrow, and for all time, this plant is used as an offering to the Earth and back to the Father Spirit.

ᏎᎳᏉᏱ / Selagwoyi / Warrior Plant: Representing safety and protection, this plant is carried into war and into the woods for protection.

ᎡᎵᏍᎦᎵ / Elisgali / Food for the Wise Plant: Representing wisdom and foresight, this is a very wise and spiritual plant. Providing you have a good mind and have made yourself one with everything, you can use it orally to locate anything that you may want to find. It has even been used to locate people, including fugitives or those who have gotten lost.

These seven plants can be mixed together either in cold or boiled water and used to purify oneself by washing your face and drinking a small amount. Each plant is connected to all things, and especially to God. In obtaining and preparing these plants, one must have a good and pure mind. You must be one with all creation throughout the entire process. It's not medicine if you gather them without a conscious awareness of your mental and spiritual state. For them to do their job, the plants need you to be connected to all things. They require the love and spirit of the Creator when they are being gathered and used. Your mind has to be connected in this way for God to be present in that medicine.

Here is where we can apply the twelve Keetoowah spiritual acknowledgements. I have discussed these acknowledgements previously in *Stand as One.* I elaborate on them below to explain how to become connected and to be in a good mental and spiritual state - for example, when working with medicinal plants. It's important to understand that in the practice of Indian medicine, there is no power in those herbs without this connection. The Keetoowah spiritual acknowledgements honor the sacredness of all life and all the elements we depend on for health and wellbeing.

The first three acknowledgements encompass the foundational spiritual reunification that must take place before all else:

Number One acknowledges the Spirit that is within you. This is the Spirit that the Creator gave you when you were born - a piece of His own Spirit that resides within all life.

Number Two acknowledges the Father Spirit from which your Spirit came.

Number Three acknowledges those two Spirits coming together - a reunification. To fully express this concept, you must not have any greed, selfishness, or egocentric thoughts in your mind. Any negative element can interrupt the reunification.

The next four acknowledgements encompass the elements upon which all life on Earth is based:

Number Four is the Earth, or Soil - the most powerful element. If it wasn't for the Earth, there would not be any plants. We would not have anything. The Earth is our place of origination and is the source of healing energy. The Earth gives us food, shelter, and clothes. The Soil itself can be the strongest of medicines. The Creator can help you bless a basket of Soil and it can be sprinkled around the yard and house to create a free and clear place where you live.

Number Five is the Air we breathe - another most sacred element. It is this Air that connects us to all living beings. When we honor the Air, we are in communion with all life. Air is medicine that can heal. The Earth and the Air in combination create the plants that we eat and use for healing.

Number Six is the Water that we are made up of. We are also connected to creation by Water - it sustains life and is honored as a cleansing agent. The Air and the Soil are also cleansing agents, and in combination with Water they make up the sacredness of the Earth - all of these give life to that most sacred creation.

Number Seven is the Holy Light - the Eternal Flame, or Fire. We must honor that Fire, for our warm bodies represent the heat of the Holy Light. The Eternal Flame is in the Spirit of every person. We must always have a warm welcome to all things, to all people.

The next four acknowledgements encompass the Original Peoples, or Messenger Clans, placed on the Earth by the Creator:

Number Eight is the Brown Spirit, honoring the first created the brown-skinned humans from North America.

Number Nine is the Blue Spirit, honoring those people commonly known as white from the European countries. However, you can't identify a race with the color white because that color belongs only to the Creator. The color white is synonymous with the Eternal Flame.

Number Ten is the Yellow Spirit honoring the yellow race of people, which covers the people from the Asian countries.

Number Eleven is the Black Spirit, honoring those peoples from the African continent.

The final acknowledgement encompasses all of what came before:

Number Twelve is the Eternal Energy that is formed after the reunification mentioned above - the total, comprehensive, eternal nature of spirituality that one earns by honoring the reunification of the Spirits.

These spiritual acknowledgements honor the connection between all people and all things. When acknowledged together, it is a confirmation that you are connected to everything in this universe.

As God's creations, all peoples are connected to one other. We are also all connected to the Earth and its elements because they too were created by God. It is important to stress and honor the sacredness of the Soil, this most precious element. Everything, even the first peoples, was made out of Soil and their material bodies will eventually go back to the Earth as Soil. For this reason, you must humble yourself when you walk over the land. Whether it's a meadow, prairie, or forest, humble yourself as if the grass you walk on has been fertilized by the material bodies that went back to the Earth. This is why we acknowledge the elements in relation to all people who have gone before us (yesterday), all people who are presently living (today), and all people yet to be born into this world (tomorrow, and for all time). This collective spiritual acknowledgement of the twelve concepts is the most comprehensive there is. It is made strong through the reunification of the Spirits and elements of creation - when made with a pure mind, it can't be broken. It is a responsibility that the Keetoowahs have carried forward for generations, and it represents a teaching that is meant for all people to practice. If you can fulfill the requirements in all these spiritual acknowledgements, there is nothing more powerful. It is the strongest spirituality ever.

There are other healing methods that many would consider repulsive. But I have seen them work. They require us to step outside our usual mindsets and view the act of healing as a spiritual process that does not always align with human sensibilities about what is repulsive or pleasant. For example, one time in my younger years, I witnessed my father in the process of healing an alcoholic. He asked me to find an old shoe, then take a glass of water pour it into the shoe. Then he said to pour the water back into the glass. Then he told me to find an old dried up and bleached out turtle shell and stir it into the water. After that, he instructed me to add a small amount of alcohol to the mixture and give it to the person to drink. The medicine worked - the client quit drinking. Perhaps an even more repulsive healing method I have witnessed was for nonstop hiccups. Dad instructed me to pour a glass of water into a dog's mouth and back into the glass, which he gave the client to drink. It resulted in a very successful cure.

On another occasion, a very old non-Indian man from Porum, Oklahoma, came to see me asking for kidney medicine. I gave him chips of arrow bark, or what we call *udohiyu uhnasdedla,* and told him to add them to a glass of lukewarm water. I instructed him to take a drink two times a day. It worked well for him. He told me that he knew my father, Stokes Smith. He recounted a story to me about a baby that had been born blind in his community. They asked my father if he could do something to help the baby. The man told me that he witnessed the ritual my father did, and that he was successful in giving eyesight to that baby.

On another occasion with my dad, a fourteen-year-old boy was brought to him with pain on the right side of his groin. In my father's reading, he diagnosed the pain to be an inflamed appendix. He heated his hands over a fire, and then laid them upon the area where the boy was experiencing pain. He told me later on the words he was reciting in his mind as he performed the ritual. Just before he laid his hot hands over the boy's painful area, he would summon the cooling elements: fog, frost, ice, and snow. Then he would take a good mouthful of water and spew it onto the painful area. He worked this way most of the night, and by the morning the boy was healed. The inflamed appendix did not have heat anymore. Another time, an epileptic young boy was brought to our house for my father to doctor. His seizures were so severe that his parents would have to hold him down when they occurred. If they didn't, the boy would run uncontrollably into anything - even a barbed wire fence. He would simply lose his mind. After my father did a pendulum reading, he discovered what he needed. He asked me to get the tender roots of a particular plant, and he showed me what plant it was. I did as he asked, and my father boiled these roots in a half gallon of water. He told the boy that when he senses he is going to have an epileptic spell, he should take four to five swallows of that tea. If he did this, he would not lose his mind and he would be aware of the seizure. That herb was a shock absorber. At the time, I didn't know what plant it was, but later on I learned that it was wild marijuana.

Another doctoring story: There was a young man who was affected with polio - his right arm was always twisted, and he held it over his head. He was also unable to use his right leg properly. My father built a small fire in the yard under a shade tree. When the fire was burning well, he applied cedar seedlings and heated his hands. He then laid his hands on the man's shoulder, elbow, and wrist. He did that with his ankle, hip, and his right leg. This doctoring was very successful. As time passed, you could never tell that the man had had polio - he looked normal. On another occasion, a family walked five miles to the house to ask my father for help. One of their boys had accidentally chopped his big toe off with an axe. They had placed a tourniquet below the knee to stop the bleeding. My dad walked all the way back with them, and when he got to the boy, he took out his pocketknife and took the tourniquet off. He told me he used these words to stop the bleeding: "When I came by, I saw you in your own pool of blood, but I told you: 'You're going to live on.'" Later on, somebody told me those words were in the Bible, but my father couldn't read - these words were given to him by his father. Dad asked for the severed toe and told them to bring him some spider webs. He covered the wound where the toe was cut off with webs. Then he replaced the toe and bandaged it up. That toe grew back on the boy's foot. His name was Adam Bernoski, that guy with the toe.

In my young days, I witnessed many more healing procedures. This is how I acquired my skills for healing. Dad told me that when you perform these healing methods, you relinquish everything that's in your personality. No emotions, no ego, nothing on your mind except what God gave you when you were created: God gives love and his spirit to all that comes into this world. This is the state of mind the healer is required to maintain. You become a conduit, and God does the healing.

Chapter 6

Spirit of the Fire

In the early 1980s, a Tulsa news anchor approached the traditional Keetoowah Society's council about filming a documentary that would feature our religious practices and spiritual knowledge. Seeing that this man had come to them in a good way and with an earnest intent to learn about Keetoowah traditions, the elders met to discuss the proposal. They decided that, for the very first time, they would allow video recording at the ceremonial grounds and would agree to be interviewed by the film crew about Keetoowah knowledge. This documentary is titled *Spirit of the Fire*, and it contains footage of our stomp dances and other ceremonial activities, as well as a description of our sacred wampum belts by my late brother, William Smith. Today, you can find this video on the internet if you look for it. In much the same way that this book, and my previous book, *Stand as One,* have done, the documentary represents the Keetoowah council's intention to offer our teachings for all people to ponder and learn. In this spirit, it is a resource for people to understand the meaning of ancient Keetoowah spirituality and its relevance to our times today.

But although the documentary was approved by our traditional council, there are parts that need further explanation if one is to fully understand their meaning. Shortly after the documentary was released in 1984, I was asked to give a presentation for the annual Symposium on the American Indian at Northeastern State University - the site of our former Cherokee National Female Seminary in Tahlequah, Oklahoma. In this speech, I provide background to some of the documentary footage and fill in important areas that were missed in the final cut of the film. I offer it here with minor editorial changes so that we might capture that moment in time and relate it to the other teachings in this book.

Anigaduwagi, *the Chosen People, the Keepers of the Eternal Flame*
Northeastern State University
Tahlequah, Oklahoma
April 1984

First of all, I want to express my sincere appreciation for the opportunity to share with you. I want to extend a special thanks to Carol Young and her staff, the University faculty and its president, Rodger Webb. I also want to thank the Cherokee Nation employees and Chief Ross Swimmer for their support. The presentation for this afternoon to facilitate the film, *Spirit of the Fire,* is designed to enhance your comprehension of the film in depth. The delivery of the speech will be done in the same manner as the traditional Keetoowah have done for thousands of years.

As I prepared this presentation, I recalled the names of past and present speakers. To name a few - I didn't see him in real life, but I hear him: Great Grandfather Young Pig Smith; I didn't see him in real life, but I hear him: Grandfather Redbird Smith; my father, Stokes Smith; Sam Smith, Soot Glass, Lincoln Towie, Ben Bush, William Smith, Junior Smith, Levi Pigeon, and Sam Pigeon. I feel good - I feel they are with me even now, and if you are spiritual enough you may feel their presence and may even see the shadowy figures on the stage with me. Some of the insights I'll share with you this afternoon were kept in the Keetoowah's seven medicine men circles. I recall remarks made by these seven spiritual Keetoowah medicine men. They said, "The time is not with us to tell who we are. Most of our children who have gone to school stray from the old ways, they abandoned their old law. We cry for our people even before death comes to them. The time will come when our people will stand at the crossroads of time. Many will not know what to do and we will be resting beneath the cool ground unable to help as they are dragged about by negative forces. But when the time is ripe, just as wild cherries ripen, the time will come for birds of this world to harvest the fruit - so will the time be ripe for our true identity to surface. For out of the third generation some of our very own, who will not have forsaken Our Father's law, who will not have strayed away - will bring out the truth about Keetoowah and contribute the truth to mankind. When this event takes place, there will be but a short distance to go.

Almost all of the predications have come to pass, as well as predictions from the Bible. I can't help but think about Billy Graham's book, *Approaching Hoofbeats: The Four Horsemen of the Apocalypse.* It is true we have come to the crossroads of time when we are going to commit ourselves to one side or the other, to the positive or the negative - but you must know the positive will win. I want to give tribute to the Original Keetoowahs, including the past and present leaders who so skillfully maintained their faith through all destructive elements. Keetoowahs are like diamonds, cut and polished by God, nature, and man - only seen through the small opening of the eyes shining brilliantly from the depths of the soul. From the lips of the late great Keetoowah Chief, Redbird Smith, and now from his grandson's lips, comes the words to remind me and you: "We must now get together as a race and render our contributions to mankind." Yes, we too have famous giants who lived and died for a cause, that humans may survive and not perish from this land.

Finally, after what appears to be that which is last shall be first, we come to share with you our old ways, our old law. A law that gave way to the beginning of symbolism. Today, we know of many sacred high points across this great Earth of ours. The Apaches have their sacred mountains. The Navajos have their sacred mountains. Every tribe in their country has some high point as their sacred place. Then there are monuments that commemorate the sacred mountain where God lived in the fire. We have the great Egyptian pyramids; we have the pyramids in Mexico. Almost every church has its steeples or pyramid shaped crowns; we identify these things as symbols of their faith or a coat of arms, an object to relate to - but this is a far cry from the idea of man communicating with God directly.

Due to the nature of man, almost all of the direct communication with

God was severed. One of the things that God retrieved from man was the everlasting light or holy light. He took this back because of disrespect by the recipient race, but not before the Father appeared to the ancestors of our Keetoowahs. At this appearance the Spiritual Father revealed His disappointment. He revealed a ritual suggested to our ancestors to be performed against the people who abused His Holy Light. It's said the use of cedar had its beginning with this ritual, as cedar was one of the items used in the ritual. This performance of a ritual was to place a curse on the law breakers so they would know conflict amongst themselves in the form of war, hunger, disease, and injuries from natural phenomenon of His creation. This affliction would be with the law breakers for generations and generations to come. For performing the ritual, the performer would have to leave his land to go in the westerly direction or toward the setting sun to be the world traveler. No matter what the endurance - if he never forgot the old law - God would be with him even to the end of time, that upon withdrawing the light, God would keep the light above. Until the performer is in a faraway land, and for keeping the old law, he would be given the light to keep until God returned for him and the light.

Now, in this documentary, you'll see what we believe to be the original light now known as the Eternal Flame. You'll note that it's not on a very high mountain, that it's not on a pyramid, that it's not on a pedestal, but that it's on the Mother Earth - low and humble. We are told that it was on this North American continent that the fire came to our medicine men through a voice in the fire that appeared in the sky above them. In this vision we believe that it was the great promised light. During this vision, the voice told the medicine man that they would be known as Keetoowahs and would be the chief tribe among all tribes. Instructions were given them from the vision on the method of striking the fire and the standards to be used in keeping the fire. The fire also told them to keep the fire in its natural form in the wilderness - never allow my light to be on a pedestal for show or competition again. Keep yourselves and the grounds around the fire holy. The method of preparing for holy objects was also given to them at that time. Upon receiving the fire, the new Keetoowahs placed the fire on the cross made by the creation design. The connecting of spiritual lines between the Red Man from the East and the Yellow Man from the West and the connecting of the White Man from the North and the Black Man from the South. Today, there are four logs on the altar of the Eternal Flame and the four cardinal directions honoring all humans. In the film, you'll hear my brother, William Smith, Principal Chief of the Keetoowah Society, refer to the directions as "the White roads, one into the other," which is another way of saying, "This is the non-ending respect to the human race and our Father."

The pipe you'll see in the film is believed to be the pipe used in signing the peace treaties. It may have been used in signing the infamous promise of peace from the United States government to the Indian people: "as long as the river shall flow and as long as the grass shall grow." This act is still remembered by the Keetoowahs; it was a treaty made between peoples with God as witness in honoring humans. Each item you see in the documentary has a story of its own. For example, the Sacred Belts were made by the use of the Spiritual Father's instructions about the time the Eternal Flame was given to our medicine men. A voice from the fire told them that their people were becoming weak and forgetful, that the belts must be made so people will have the opportunity to know the law. There are many secrets on the belt; one can use the belts to learn the way of life here on Earth. All of our basics in medicines and doctoring come built on this rock-solid foundation. These belts were in existence when Sir Alexander Cuming first arrived in the Cherokee country from Britain in the early 1700s. It was at this time that the Keetoowahs saw so many of their people bow down before a man. Before, they bowed to their God, but now they were bowing down before a man. The old law keepers saw the writing on the wall. They decided to move on with their belts and with their identity and with their sacred fire to continue their world travel towards the setting sun - to what would soon be called Indian Territory, and later, Oklahoma. After all, this was their Spiritual Father's instructions in the first place. The Keetowahs gave notice to all others, but it was too late - the change and damage had already taken place.

At the request of Cherokee Nation Principal Chief Wilma Mankiller, on October 1, 1982, anthropologist Dr. Duane King wrote to me with an account of a Keetoowah sacred belt from Mr. Lloyd Sequoyah from the Eastern Band of Cherokees in North Carolina. When the happenings described by Mr. Sequoyah took place, the Keetoowahs were already in what is now known as Fort Smith and Van Buren, Arkansas. This is his account, as told by Dr. King:

> *In the fall of 1979, Lloyd Sequoyah, a respected Tribal Elder and medicine man from the Big Cove community of the Qualla boundary, related to me a story which he heard as a boy concerning a sacred belt which originated about the same time as the American Revolution. He said the belt was taken to Indian Territory during the removal period. At the time Lloyd told the story to me, he was in his late 70s and is now deceased. Lloyd Sequoyah was one of the plaintiffs in a lawsuit against the Tennessee Valley Authority filed by the Eastern Band of Cherokees Indians in an effort to prevent flooding of the Little Tennessee Valley by the Tellico Reservoir. This valley holds a number of important sites in Cherokee culture and mythology, including Echota, Citico, Toqua, Tenasi, Tomotley, Tuskegee, Mialoquo, Kahite, Coyatee.*
>
> *The story told by Lloyd Sequoyah is best as I can remember. It is as follows: Shortly after the outbreak of the American Revolution, the Cherokee Nation was in a state of disarray. Cherokee war parties attempted unsuccessfully to dislodge white settlers in what is now upper eastern Tennessee. In July of 1776, War Parties under Dragging Canoe (Tsiyu Gansini) were defeated at the Battle of Island Flats with heavy losses. Old Abraham of Chilhowie and The Raven of Echota withdrew their War Parties from the siege of Fort Caswell and Carter's Valley after learning of Dragging Canoe's defeat. Within a few months, punitive expeditions of whites from the Virginian frontier entered the Cherokee Nation and destroyed most of the towns on the Little Tennessee River. Echota was spared in a conciliatory gesture because the whites believed that at least one of the residents there had not favored the recent war.*
>
> *In a meeting in the Echota Town House, when the remainder of the*

Cherokee Nation was in a state of devastation, many people held the belief that the Cherokee might soon be destroyed as a people. A religious leader, speaking to the group that had assembled, blamed the problems on the Cherokees themselves. He said that their failure to adhere to the ancient laws and beliefs resulted in their misfortune, including the military defeats at the hands of the whites. Their use of alcohol was one example of their failure to abide by ancient traditions.

At this meeting, the religious leader produced a sacred belt which was approximately six feet in length and a hand breadth in width. He said that the meaning of the belt was so clear, that anyone could understand it. The belt was made from black and white shell beads, approximately three-eighths to one-half inches in length, and one-quarter inch in diameter. At one end of the belt were two human figures with hands clasped. These, he said, represented people in the bond of friendship embarking in life's journey. At the other end of the belt was a checked design representing heaven. A white strip of beads ran almost the entire length of the belt, bordered on each side by black strips of beads. The white strip, he said, indicated the path that people should follow. Lloyd referred to this "straight and narrow path" as the Duyukta. I have also heard this word used in other contexts and translated variously as "righteous," "just," and "without error." To my knowledge, there is no anonym for this word in Cherokee. If someone is not living according to the religious moral code, it is frequently said, "Gesti duyukta yinedaneha" [they are not following the righteous path]. The black areas, he said, represented the ways man sometimes wanders during life's course. The prophet told the people assembled in the Echota Town House that the problems which had befallen them resulted from their wanderings into these evil ways. He instructed them to seek a true course in life. Upon finishing the explanations, he hung the belt on a cross beam between two of the main supports in the Town House.

He encouraged the people to remember the message of the belt. He said that as long as the ground on which he stood survived so too would the Cherokee people. But when the ground and the belt were destroyed, the existence of the Cherokees as a distinct people would end. When the prophet stepped away from the belt it ignited with no apparent source for the flame. The belt burned from one end to the other. The people became frightened because they thought the prophesy concerning the destruction of the Cherokee people was about to come true. But, when the fire went out and they examined the belt and couldn't find any evidence of fire damage, either to the strings or the beads, this gave them greater faith in the words of the prophet and in the chances of the Cherokee people to endure any adversity.

Lloyd Sequoyah did not know the fate of the belt. He knew that it had been taken to Oklahoma, but having received no further word about it, believed it had either been destroyed or fallen out of Cherokee hands. For this reason, he felt that it was extremely important that the land where the Echota Town House formally stood be protected. For that reason, he was an active participant in the lawsuit against the Tennessee Valley Authority.

We give special thanks to Duane King, Deputy Chief Wilma Mankiller, and Principal Chief Ross Swimmer. We believe that the Principal Chief, Ross Swimmer, is acting in the role predicted over a hundred years ago. Without him, we know not which group would have been representing the Keetoowahs. A sincere tribute is given to our Chief for giving us the opportunity to rightfully represent our way of life, our culture, and the culture of all our people.

You can see the sacred belt from Lloyd Sequoyah's account in the *Spirit of the Fire* documentary, wherein my late brother William describes the seven Keetoowah wampum belts. We call it the White Road belt, and I also describe it in my first book. It is pictured here with my father, Stokes Smith, around his neck. The next photograph shows me at our ceremonial

My father, Stokes Smith, with Keetoowah wampum belts.
Photo credit: Paul Rodgers

Me interpreting the White Road wampum belt at the Keetoowah ceremonial grounds. Photo credit: Suzie Barnoski

grounds describing the White Road belt some time ago. The sacred message of this belt is profound, yet, as the prophet in Mr. Sequoyah's account said, "the meaning of the belt [is] so clear, that anyone [can] understand it." To walk in the White Path with nothing but love for all creation is how the Creator instructed us to live. This message is the foundation of our Original Teachings.

Chapter 7

Clans

Originally, there were four clans of the earth - the Brown Clan, the Blue Clan, the Black Clan, and the Yellow Clan. These original clans are known as the messengers. This concept of messenger is derived from how we understand medicine as a spiritual practice. In our practice of medicine, we always address the four cardinal directions, represented by each of one of these messenger clans. They are called the head messengers, or the Creator's messengers, and they represent the four peoples who originally journeyed this earth as the first human creations. The concept, or philosophy, behind this is that of unity in spite of difference. It teaches one to be receptive toward others and to accept difference as a part of Creation, but also that the core human spirit is the same regardless of color or complexion. What we call the "lower clans" are those that our Cherokee people use to organize our ceremonial practices and that help give meaning to our people's roles based on admired animal traits. These are known as the Seven Clans, and they are not the same as the Original Messenger Clans.

The story goes that Cherokees once had twelve clans. They lived together in another land from where we are now. But because conditions in that world had become so corrupt, the Creator instructed them to leave. Seven clans obeyed the Creator's command, but the other five did not leave this particular area. And so, in our country, our America, we have seven recognized clans. Some of our Iroquoian relatives have only three clans in their tribe. For many Indian nations, clan systems help the people to model their personality traits on the teachers of the natural world, specifically animals. For the Keetoowah, the clans are matrilineal - one inherits their clan from their mother. This matrilineal system of animal representations stresses the teachings of nonhuman beings and the special status of women in Cherokee society. For millennia, it has provided the Keetoowah people with moral guidelines and has informed our system of governance. The clan system also provides guidelines for marriage - a person can only marry someone outside of their clan. For generations, these guidelines have assured Cherokees a genetically sound posterity. In the old country - our Cherokee homelands - clan guidelines were strictly, perhaps sacredly, followed from town to town, although each town functioned independently. Obedience to clan guidelines was commonplace and universally adopted by all who were Keetoowah. At its best, the clan system served as an adhesive for unity and allegiance that kept the total nation connected.

Many historians and anthropologists have written about the Blood Law that was once practiced in association with the clan system, but I feel like they make too much of it. It was not one of the guiding principles of the system. On a simple level, we can relate it to the infamous feud between the Hatfields and the McCoys, where one family was wronged by another and lives were taken to get revenge - like "an eye for an eye." Within some Indian nations, this got out of hand. The Iroquois Confederacy corrected for this by creating the Six Nations councils that took responsibility for settling clan disputes. Another element to the Blood Law wasn't so much about family feuds, but rather about replacing an individual who was lost with someone who could take on the deceased person's roles in the community. This didn't just happen within the tribe, it happened in our interactions with other tribes, too. For example, if a Shawnee war party kidnapped or killed a young boy, then our people would go to capture a boy from the Shawnee. That boy was adopted by our people and turned over to a clan mother who would teach him about his community roles and responsibilities as a member of that clan. So, there's more to the way this law was practiced than just revenging someone's death. It was an acknowledgement of the loss that the community suffered - the replacement was seen to help restore balance.

Each clan has a specialty - a strong personality or philosophical approach to life. The ultimate goal is for each person to utilize these specialties, to learn from them and employ them in their life. If a person can equip oneself with the specialties of all the clans - modeling the animal traits and characteristics in their actions and behaviors - they become a very strong person. Doing so also leads a person toward the uppermost way, which is suggested by our name, *Gaduwagi*. This is not saying that a person should take on multiple personalities or sacrifice their integrity. Rather, it's saying that a person can incorporate multiple traits and characteristics drawn from animal teachers in the way they live their life. Clearly, the clans are for human growth and spiritual duty. For those who take their clan seriously, they are used for structuring one's life and for answering questions such as: Who am I? and What is my purpose? In the truest sense, the clans play a major role in shaping one's nature in developing human attributes.

For instance, the Bear specializes in strength due to their strong physical statures. The Wolf teaches family values and cooperation - they live and hunt together in packs. The Panther has the specialty to be able to maneuver or get through things. The specialty of the Birds of Prey or the Big Hawks is that they have good vision and can see far away. The Little Birds have societal and relational strengths. They can be together in close proximity in the same environment without any adverse effect - they still relate well to each other. The strength of the of the Deer is fleetness and sensitivity - their keen senses. The Small Prairie Animals exist out in the open without much protection, but they can conceal themselves by blending into their environment. Their sensitivity is much stronger than the Deer, who uses its fleetness to go from one place to another in a short time. These animals make up our representatives of the Seven Clans. Somewhere down the line the anthropologists assigned them different English names, like "Wild Potato" and "Long Hair," but the animals above describe the original teachings of the clans. My elders told me that long ago, the people saw various animals demonstrate attributes and characteristics that helped them to obey and follow what the Creator had designed for them. The animals conducted themselves in a manner that indicated they knew their proper purpose in life. The animals also show their ability to be in harmony with the elements and the natural order of the world. And so, the people sought to honor the animals' behaviors.

At the ceremonial grounds, the Seven Clans are used to govern participation in communions and funerals, or when the clans are summoned to the fire for spiritual participation. Today, if one does not know their clan, they are not permitted to participate in some of these activities. But, despite this, we should not think of the clan system as a way to exclude our own people. I think a person can have a clan even if they don't inherit it directly from their mother. They could look to their ancestors, perhaps their father's mother, or someone further back. One could even go back to the higher level and associate with one of the Original Messenger Clans.

Keetoowah teachings say that we are not to lose or forget our clan - as if a time will come that we must demonstrate that we know our clan; that it will be necessary to know how to live your life in a manner that is designated for you. They also teach that all clans are equal; no single clan is superior or more important than the others. Clan-to-clan allegiance is continuously emphasized and is embroidered into one of the wampum belts, which are used to relate laws that were set forth by the Creator. In essence, the clans have a close and sacred connection to the Creator. As denoted in the descriptions below, there are seven arbors at the ceremonial grounds that are arranged circling the fire counterclockwise from the southwest around to the northwest. The space to the west is left open.

This knowledge was given to us by our Keetoowah elders, and much of it has been written down by my late brother, Benny Smith. He designed for the Cherokee Nation a chart with the following analysis of the clans and their names in the Cherokee language. I present it here because there has been much erosion of the Original Teachings of the clans. It is important to understand the original thought behind them, and also to not lose sight of the Creator's Original Messenger Clans, which represent a higher law and to which everyone belongs.

Southwest

ᎠᏂᎪᏓᎨᏫ / *anigodagewi* / Small Prairie Animal Clan

This clan has perhaps the broadest description and representation of the animal world. *Anigodagewi* resembles several other Cherokee words and phrases. These similarities readily suggest a variety of meanings. In Cherokee, *agodi* denotes a prairie, and there is little doubt that the *godi* in the clan name refers to this. The name, therefore, refers to animals that live on the prairie, or savannah. In some English translations, *anigodagewi* is described as the Wild Potato Clan, which is void of any animal correlation but also might signal the environment where this plant grows. *Gewi* refers to those small creatures of the prairie who have a sparse covering of hair surrounding the head or eye areas. To say *"agewi"* describes someone without eyebrows or hair covering about the head. It seems very logical that the broad array of smaller animals that make the open prairie their home are collectively the animals that symbolically represent the *anigodagewi,* or Wild Potato Clan.

Related words: *Usgewi,* meaning the Wild Potato plant; *akewi,* the Cherokee word for blind; *agewi,* a description of spare or no hair covering; *agodi,* the Cherokee word for prairie.

South

ᎠᏂᏩᏯ / *aniwaya* / Wolf Clan

The name for the Wolf Clan is clearly taken from the wolf. *Waya,* or *wahya,* is the Cherokee word for wolf. When we hear a wolf howl, we say, "*wahya nigawe.*" To say that someone is calling would be *wahyani.* Therefore, the wolf is named by the sounds he makes and is the symbolic animal that represents *aniwaya,* the Wolf Clan.

Related words: Wahyani can have multiple meanings, depending on the context: One can mean "to call for," another can mean "he has gone to get him," and yet another can mean that a person has taken a partner, or accepted someone into the family, adopted a child, and so on.

East

DhYGᏔ / *anigilohi* / Panther Clan

For Cherokee speakers, the name for this clan has an animal sound or "ring" to it. English translations for this clan have ranged from "Long Hair" to "Twister" to "Stranger" Clan. An elder (my father, the late Stokes Smith) recalled hearing the word *anigilo* in reference to the lions *(anitlvdatsi)*. Animals in the lion family, including the mountain lion, cougar, panther, and even the African lion (the one with the long heavy mane about the neck), have a habit of lying along high places - on trees, ledges, and cliffs - that give them a vantage point to observe all that passes beneath them. *Unigilo* means "they are perched, or above ground." *Danigo'i* means "they lay (at ground level) often." *Anitlvdatsi* (lions) are given the unique credit for both being perched and laying above ground level that is not afforded most animals. The sounds and syllables of these two verbs are combined to form *gilo*. This oral history strongly suggests that the lions are the symbolic animals that represent the clan *anigilohi.*

Related words: *Danigo'i,* meaning "they lay there often;" *ugilo,* meaning "they are perched upon often;" *kilo,* meaning "stranger;" and *unigilowadego,* meaning "they are often upon something."

Northeast

DhᎣᏗ / *aniwodi* / Hawk Clan

The name for this clan strongly suggests that it is taken from an animal's appearance. The English translation is often noted as the Paint Clan, likely due to the word *uwodi,* which is the name for a red powder that is highly regarded and is used as medicine during the most extreme times of human endeavors. But *uwodi* does not have an animal correlation. Additionally, there are several other words that bear consideration in understanding the name of this clan: First, the name given to the hawk is *tawodi.* This name is derived from the word *atawodi,* meaning "it is combed" (such as in the appearance of birds of prey). Second, the Cherokee word for pretty is *uwoduhi.* We can interpret the similar sounds of these words to refer to the neatly combed look and stately posture of birds of prey

- these qualities were deemed beautiful by our ancestors. In this analysis, the birds of prey seem to be the most likely representations of *aniwodi* - what we call the Hawk Clan.

Related words: *Uwoduhi,* meaning "pretty;" *atawodi,* meaning "it is combed;" *tawodi,* the Cherokee name for the hawk. *Uwodi* is the name of a red powder that is highly regarded and is used as medicine in dire conditions. *Udowodi* is the finely finished deer skin medicine bag in which *uwodi* is kept, along with other medicines.

North

ᎠᏂᏥᏍᏆ / *anitsisqua* / Bird Clan

The name for the Bird Clan clearly designates the small birds as the representatives for this clan. The Cherokee word for bird is *tsisqua.* The name appears to be derived from *unisquisda,* a word meaning "many" (as in an abundance of). For instance, the name given to blackbirds is *anisquilisda,* perhaps because these small birds flock in great numbers. Such birds can coexist harmoniously in close quarters, eating together and sharing shelter. It is said that many of these types of birds mate for life and return each season to the same nesting place. For these reasons, Cherokee people regard the smaller birds as exhibiting very high moral and relational values.

Related words: *Tsisqua,* meaning "bird;" *squisda,* meaning "many," or "an abundance of."

Northwest

ᎠᏂᎠᏫ / *aniawi* / Deer Clan

This clan name also clearly refers to a specific animal - the Deer. *Awi,* as well as *ahawi* and *ahawa,* mean "deer." The Elk, Buffalo, Antelope and other hooved animals share traits and characteristics with the Deer. These animals have a fleeing instinct, keen senses, and great speed and endurance. *Uwi* is an old Cherokee word that refers to the lower leg with the hoof still attached. These were used as medicine to doctor horses, dogs, and other domesticated animals for various physical conditioning treatments or to achieve improved performance. Thus, the Deer and their hooved relatives are the symbolic representatives for *aniawi,* the Deer Clan.

Related words: *Awi, ahawi,* and *ahawa* are all words for deer. *Uwi* is the word for the lower leg parts of an animal, including the hoof, that can be used as medicine.

Animals are some of our many teachers in this world, and this is why our ancestors placed them as representatives of the Seven Clans. Animals observe their surroundings and are in harmony with their environment. They know their own nature, as well as when and how to do things to survive, like building a nest or preparing for the winter. In other words, they obey the Creator's instructions much better than humans. As humans, we may be self-aware and intelligent, but we would do well to emulate the behavior and virtues of non-human animals.

Through the marriage guidelines, the clan system also encouraged the development of well-rounded individuals in our society. Marrying a person outside of one's clan not only served a genetic purpose, but also served to spread the various traits of each clan evenly across the society by creating kinship responsibilities and fostering knowledge of the different clan traits.

Consider an individual who is observant of all the characteristic strengths of the Seven Clans. This would be a very prestigious type person. They would have the ability to know and embody the natures of each clan, including the ability to relate well to all the people of various clans. In modern times, I've observed our people who go off and work in another geographical location and they fit into those communities really well. I think that shows they are utilizing all those human traits and characteristics that are positive. The clan system teaches acceptance, interpersonal harmony, and how to understand the nature of another person. Through this system, even if you are not of the Wolf Clan, if you know its traits and characteristics, you can very easily strengthen someone who is by admiring them or saying something positive about their specialty.

One of the biggest downfalls to our society occurred within a few generations when our clan system was uprooted and eroded through intermarriage with European people - the English, the Spanish, Irish, Germans, and French. It wasn't so much about mixing with other races as it was about not carrying forward the teachings of the clan system - the assimilation of our people away from what had allowed us to prosper for so long. The traditionalists, the ones that did not intermarry, could see this erosion taking place. In a sense, that just gave them a stronger incentive to hold on to the old ways. This is attributed to the *Anigaduwagi*, the Keetoowahs. They held on to their own ways because they saw what was happening.

The bylaws of the Keetoowah Society are based on the number seven. We have the Seven Sacred Wampum Belts, the Seven Clans, and the Seven Medicine Men from each clan. The Seven Medicine Men must try to be as pure as an angel - a divine being from above. It's like they entertain seven angels through this work. There are Seven Sacred Plants that they use to make a tea, which is our Holy Water. After a special ceremonial dance, everyone takes this medicine to purify themselves. And lastly, we believe in the Seven Heavens of the afterlife where our spirits go when we leave this world. As you can see, seven is one of our sacred numbers. Our people sometimes say, "Go seven strong." This means that the strengths of all the Seven Clans can be used by one individual. It shows how our clan system serves the people in many ways. We should strive to uphold it in our everyday actions.

Epilogue

I would like to end with a final acknowledgement of the ancestors. Long before the Trail of Tears, the spiritual people of the Keetoowah Society were capable and intelligent enough to foresee the future. They always referred to a time in the past when our people were maybe on this continent, maybe on another continent - that they had one of the greatest and strongest civilizations. They were strong, sturdy, and big. They also were able to know about other continents the world over, as well as beyond this earth - the universe, the stars, and the different planets that may have life. This was a far-reaching interpretation of their existence.

At that time, they said our people would one day lose the power that they had because they will create imagery of their own. This would be a manmade concept of spirituality. For that reason, they decided that they had to create something visible - audiovisual aids - for the people who are not yet born to learn from, because their struggle in life would be tremendous. They foresaw that their people would be mistreated, and they knew that they would be unable to help because they would long be gone from this earthly world. However, they knew that if the people could learn from what they created - the sacred wampum belts - this would give them the information they needed about the sacredness of the earth and to do the right things: to think right, to do right, to follow the Original Teachings of spirituality that will lead them to life after death. These belts were the scriptures of the old times. Some of those sacred belts are older than the

Bible. They teach good fundamental values.

Once a person has learned the values of these belts, they have accomplished what the ancestors desired. The belts are not as valuable if one has truly learned the teachings. And these are the concepts that we pass on to the people who we try to take care of today. And when I say "the people," I mean **all** people. The spirits of the past. The present people of this world. If there is life on other planets, we include that. And we also have the future to consider. We consider the people that are not yet born in hopes that they will learn. This is the same as our ancestors did for us when they created relics to remind us of the true spirituality. So, we honor all things that are coming in the future. It had to be many hundred years before the coming of the Son of God, the Christ, when these concepts were developed. And He came because people had abandoned the true spirituality. He came to renew all of these important spiritual values on this earth. But even then, some people were misled, and they are still functioning in the dark. So, we consider the people who are on their way to be born into this world.

We want their spirits to learn the truth, and the truth will free them.

Anigaduwagi Observations

by Benny Smith

The following is what I recall hearing from *Anigaduwagi* elders.

ᎡᎶᎯ ᏄᏍᏗᏓᏅ ᎥᏍᏊ ᎥᎳᎩᏰᎦ ᎪᏍᏓᏭ ᏂᎦᏓ ᎢᎩᏥ.

Elohi nusdidanv vsquu vlagiyega kosdawu nigada igitsi.

I am planted in the natural order of the world; dust (earth) is the mother to everything (all others: plants, stones, animals, etc.).

ᎠᏎᏃ ᎠᎩᏆᏛᏗ ᏂᎦᏓᏭ ᎪᎱᏍᏗ ᏗᎦᏓᏛᏂ ᎤᏠᏯᏭ ᏓᏰᎦᏙᎴᏅᎯ ᎡᎶᎯ ᏥᏕᎯ ᏂᏧᎳᎭᏭ ᏕᏓᏓᎵᎮᎵᏍᎪ ᎠᎴ ᏕᏓᏓᏍᎦᏂᎰ ᎠᎴ ᏙᏗᏟᏬᎪ.

Aseno agiquadvdi nigadawu gohusdi digadadvni utloyawu dayegadolenvhi elohi tsidehi nitsulahawu dedadalihelisgo ale dedadasganiho ale doditliwogo.

I must see, we are all related. We have a beginning or an origin that is much the same because we all exist in this world - together we have joy, grief (crying), and we die.

ᎡᎶᎯ ᎦᎸᎾᏓ ᎠᎴ ᎡᎶᎯ ᎦᏙᎯ ᎨᏒ ᏳᏚᎾᏠᏏ ᎢᎦᎵᏍᏕᎵᏙᏗ ᎠᏙᏛᏍᎩ ᏂᎦᏓ ᎢᎦᎵᏍᏕᎵᏙᏗ.

Elohi galvladi ale elohi gadohi gesv yudunadlosi igalisdelidodi adotvsgi nigada igalisdelidodi.

Only when the Above World and the Earth World come together and collaborate can that which we need to help ourselves be made and/or produce all that is about us.

ᎠᏆᏅᏔ ᎾᏍᎩ ᏂᎪᎵᏍᏗᏍᎪ ᏜᏃ ᎢᏳᏙᎴᏅᏓᏭ ᏄᏍᏗᏓᏅ ᎠᏆᏕᎵᏍᏆᏍᏗ ᏲᎦᎦᎦ.

Aquanta nasgi nigolisdisgo dlano iyudolenvdawu nusdidanv aquadelisquasdi yogagaga.

I know that this happens, I need not study, learn, or doubt this is so.

ᏅᏓ ᏗᎧᎸᎩ ᎡᎶᎯ ᏗᎦᎵᏍᎬ ᏝᏎ ᎢᎦᏕᎳᎰᎯᏍᏗ ᎪᎵᏍᎩ ᏱᎩ?

Nvda dikalvgi elohi digalisgv tlase igadelahohisdi golisgi yigi?

The sun comes up and passes over all during the day. Is there any purpose to know why?

ᎦᏓᏠᏍᎪ ᎾᎪᎲᏍᏗ ᏙᎦᏓᏛᏗ ᎥᎾᏙ ᏕᎦᎶᏏᏍᎬ ᎪᎨ ᎤᎶᎪᎯ ᎪᎳ ᎠᎴ ᏕᎦᏅᎪᎬ ᎠᏎᏃ ᏓᏤᎶ ᎤᏃᎯᏳᏐ ᎤᎾᏛᏄᏫ ᏐᏃ ᎨᏐ.

Gadatlosgo nagohvsdi dogadadvdi vnado degalosisgv goge ulogohi gola ale deganvgogv aseno datselo unohiyuso unadvnuwi sono geso.

I am made aware that my earthly relatives know the approaching and passing of summer, autumn, winter and spring, but better than me they obey and know when to prepare for seasonal commands.

ᎤᏠᏯᏊ ᎪᎱᏍᏗ ᏰᎦᏕᏏᏓ ᏫᏗᏲᎦ ᎢᎦᎢᎫ ᏰᏫᏗᎵᏬᏣᏃ ᎪᏍᏛ ᎢᎩᎩᏑ ᏫᏣᏨᏍᏗ.

Utloyaqu gohusdi yegadesida widiyoga igaigu yewidiliwotsano kosdv igigisu witsatsvsdi.

We all, likewise, can be thrown about by something until we are broken and die. Then we return to dust, the Mother of All.

ᎬᏗ ᏥᎪᏩᏘᏍᎪ ᎪᎲᏍᏓ ᏗᎫᎥᎦᎣᏛᏓ ᏳᎾᏛᏗ ᎠᏁᏩᏕᎬ ᎠᏯᏃ ᎠᏆᏛ ᏗᎨᏐ ᎭᎸ ᏕᎦᏕᎴᏍᏆᏍᎨᏍᏗ ᎠᎴ ᎠᏆᏁᎵᏏ ᎨᎮᏍᏗ ᎠᎴ ᏓᏆᏘᎾ ᎡᏍᏗᏍ.

Gvdi tsigowatisgo gohvsda diguvgaodvda yunadvdi anewadegv ayano aquadv digeso halv degadelisquasgesdi ale aquanelisi gehesdi ale daquatina esdis.

It is clear, I can see that my relatives know what they are to do during life, but me I have to find where and what to learn, to have a mate, or to have off-spring.

ᎪᎱᏍᏗ ᏗᏋᎾ ᏫᏟᎢᎦᎢ ᎠᏂ ᏌᎹᏙ ᎤᎾᏙ ᏳᏃᏛᏗ ᎠᏯᏃ ᎠᎩᏍᏗᏰᏍᏗᏍᎪ ᏯᏆᏛᏗ.

Gohusdi diquvna witli'iga'i ani samado unado yunodvdi ayano agisdiyesdisgo yaquadvdi.

My relatives are much smarter; they know what they are to do. But me, I must struggle with the decisions of life.

Ꮭ ᏰᎵ ᏰᎦᎠ ᎦᏥᎪᎾᏗᏍᎬ ᎾᎾ ᏛᏁᎲ ᎪᎱᏍᏗ ᏗᏋᎾ ᏚᏳᏚ ᎮᎾ ᎾᎾᏛᏁ ᎠᏯᏃ ᎠᏎ ᏂᎬᎾᏛ ᎠᎩᏠᏯᏍᏗ ᎠᎴ ᏂᎦᏓ ᎦᏥᏠᏲᏍᏗ ᏂᎦᏛᏁᎲ ᎩᎳᏃ ᎤᎵᏍᎨᏗ ᏫᏂᎦᎵᏍᏗ ᎨᎥ ᎨᏏᏕᎬ.

Tla yeli yega'a gatsigonadisgv nana dvnehv gohusdi diquvna duyudu hena nanadvne ayano ase nigvnadv agitloyasdi ale nigada gatsitloyosdi nigadvnehv gilano ulisgedi winigalisdi ge'v gesidegv.

It is not enough for me to see what my relatives do in their life is right. For me, I must include all (the whole) and include all my relatives for their sacredness in my living.

Afterword

It has been a great honor to help my elder and friend, Crosslin Smith, publish the teachings reflected in this book and in his previous book, *Stand as One.* In reflecting on his request for me to contribute some words, I am humbled. In what follows, I describe our work together - on his two books, as well as on other related projects - and offer some thoughts on the significance of this work, both personally and broadly.

Crosslin and I first met in 2008 at Stokes' Ceremonial Grounds near Vian, Oklahoma. The grounds are named for his father, Stokes Smith, and they're about a hundred yards from Crosslin's homestead. The event was the annual ceremonial stomp dance in honor of Chief Redbird Smith's birthday on July nineteenth. Redbird, Crosslin's grandfather, was a highly respected Keetoowah spiritual and political leader and is one of the most well-known figures in Cherokee history. On that summer evening, I approached Crosslin for his advice and sought his support for a tribal ethnobotany project that I had been conducting as an employee of the Cherokee Nation Natural Resources Department. He agreed to meet at a later time to discuss things in more detail. Over time, and as our friendship and his trust in me grew, he became the project's biggest supporter.

Working with Cherokee Nation staff to enlist the support and participation of other renowned elders and knowledge-keepers, this project eventually led to the formation of the Cherokee Nation Medicine Keepers, to which Crosslin now serves as Spiritual Advisor. In our most recent work with the Medicine Keepers and Cherokee Nation staff, we are training five Cherokee students in traditional and Western scientific knowledge of plants and ecosystems in the Cherokee Nation. Crosslin has provided invaluable mentorship to me, staff, and the students in the course of this work, and the project would be greatly diminished without it. The entire effort is indebted to his wisdom and support of our goals to perpetuate Cherokee knowledge and ways of being. This book is an eagerly awaited addition to our curriculum, of which *Stand as One* is already a part.

Crosslin is a renowned medicine man and continues this practice as one in a long line of influential healers and Keetoowah leaders. Although he stands on the shoulders of his ancestors, his story is distinctive and remarkable. His traditional upbringing and the early experiences that defined him as a gifted individual have earned him a reputation far and wide as one of the strongest healers around. The responsibility of being a healer comes with a burden that Crosslin carries effortlessly and out of love for his people and all humankind. Although the practice of traditional medicine is certainly about healing physical ailments, it is also about providing culturally and spiritually grounded counsel to his patients that extends beyond the realm of the physical and works to instill pride and positive leadership qualities. People apply this counsel to their own lives as well as the lives of others; thus, the "ripple effect" of Crosslin's work is significant, considering that his clientele would easily include thousands of individuals over his lifetime. The value of this from a Cherokee perspective is undeniably profound. Crosslin has provided leadership and spiritual assistance to nearly every contemporary Cherokee Nation administration. Further, his healing abilities are known and respected throughout the world by leaders and other healers from numerous nations and cultures.

When it was released in 2018, *Stand as One* marked the first time Keetoowah Cherokee spiritual teachings had been printed and thus made available for those outside the Keetoowah Society to learn without visiting the ceremonial grounds. In alignment with the original instructions from the Creator, Crosslin wished to make them available for all people to contemplate and incorporate into their lives amid the increasingly alienated world in which we find ourselves today. I was aware of his intent to publish a book of this nature shortly after we first met. Crosslin's friend, Dr. Marial Martyn, had been interviewing him from January 2009 to July 2010, and the transcripts from those interviews make up the bulk of *Stand as One.* Due to unforeseen circumstances, Marial was unable to complete the project. When Crosslin called me in November of 2016 to ask if I would help him finish it, I unhesitatingly agreed, understanding the importance and urgency of this request.

I soon started the process of compiling, editing, and giving structure to what would become the book manuscript out of Marial's transcripts, as well as drawing from numerous other materials Crosslin had given me. Although this process challenged me out of concern for accurately representing the material, it was also revelatory: In the course of the work, I realized that Crosslin has been relating to me the stories in the book ever since we first met. Being familiar with many of the teachings therein eased the process and filled in areas that I had previously missed or forgotten. And yet, I can't understate the learning process this work has been for me. In closely reading and contemplating his words, and through our conversations in person and over the phone about the manuscript drafts, I've come to know my friend and his life purpose even more. I am fortunate and blessed to do this work, which has deeply influenced how I navigate life and nurture my own spiritual and relational growth.

As for publishers, Crosslin initially asked my opinion on this, having published my own book in 2015 with the University of Minnesota Press. After approaching another university press about the manuscript, I realized that this didn't feel right - my limited experience with this corner of the publishing world didn't seem to fit the nature and intent behind this work. Further, Crosslin wished to retain the copyright to the work in full, which I knew might clash with academic publishing practices. Ultimately, through Marial's connection, we approached John Pruit of Dog Soldier Press to publish *Stand as One.*

A small, independently owned company out of Taos, New Mexico, John founded Dog Soldier Press "to focus the light of public attention on the accomplishments of people, who...take a stand and commit themselves to a greater good." John's response was enthusiastic, and it has been a great pleasure to work with him throughout the process for both books. I felt further comforted in this direction by Crosslin's confidence - after receiving an email reply from John that indicated his strong interest in publishing *Stand as One,* I called Crosslin and asked him what he thought. Following a short pause in which Crosslin spiritually "looked into it," he said, definitively, "that's the one." Recognizing the significance of the book's release to Crosslin and the family, John hand-delivered boxes of the first printing of *Stand as One* to Crosslin in December 2018, traveling from Taos to Vian, Oklahoma using his personal expenses.

This book, *Original Teachings,* is intended to be a companion to *Stand as One,* and the process has also been a team effort. A longtime friend of Crosslin who studied traditional medicine under him, Dr. Jody Noe, traveled from Connecticut to record and transcribe the material for the manuscript. Out of these transcriptions, which had already been organized into chapters by Crosslin, the manuscript began to take shape. Additionally, at Crosslin's request, Jody and I worked to incorporate materials from his late brother, Benny Smith, which appear throughout the text. An excerpt of Benny's writings, *Anigaduwagi* Observations, is included as a stand-alone contribution to this book. In this way, Crosslin honors the close relationship he had with his younger brother by including their shared knowledge herein, which they spent much time discussing and philosophizing about when they could.

The cover concepts for both books are from Crosslin. They depict the four Original Messenger peoples represented by the colors brown, blue, yellow, and black, with the sacred eternal flame in the center. Publication editor Ananda Sundari lent her excellent graphic design skills for the cover of *Stand as One.* The book you hold in your hand is graced with the artwork of Cherokee National Treasure, Mary HorseChief. To many Native peoples, east is the primary point of reference when you are looking at a two-dimensional representation of the directions. This is in contrast to the dominant Euro-Western point of reference that places north at the top of the page. So, as Crosslin relates to us, this representation honors all people, starting with Brown to the east, Blue to the north, Yellow to the west, and Black to the south. These cover designs offer another profound Keetoowah lesson - expressed visually - that we must honor all people in all that we do. It reminds us that we are all connected through the sacred fire that burns within us. The warmth of our bodies comes from the spirit of life that was given to everyone by the Creator when they were born.

In the cover for *Original Teachings,* Crosslin wanted to show that the colors representing the four Original Messenger peoples do not stop at some unknown point beyond the horizon. Rather, they continue around our Mother Earth to meet back at the center. This is where the sacred fire resides, and it is encompassed by a white square, which represents the Creator. Mary HorseChief's artwork beautifully portrays this teaching that Crosslin retained from his elder Keetoowah ceremonial leaders. The four logs positioned around the sacred fire at the four cardinal directions represent projections of prayer that envelop the earth and return to the source of life itself. What better way to understand how we are all connected to each other, the Creator, the sacred fire, and the earth?

We could view such foundational teachings as the structure that holds within it many of the details that Crosslin provides in *Original Teachings* and *Stand as One*. In each, he recounts Keetoowah knowledge, experience, and stories from ancient times to the present, illuminating our connections to one another as human beings and emphasizing the profound responsibility that Keetoowah people have had to live and maintain the Creator's Original Instructions. Through these books, Crosslin also fulfills a prophecy he heard from his elders that one day the world will learn the truth about the Keetoowah faith and the teachings it contains. In doing so, Crosslin is helping to ensure that we don't lose sight of the Original Bylaws that express love for *the spirit* in oneself and in all people, love for the Creator, and love for the four sacred elements of fire, water, soil, and air that support and unite all life on Earth. This is the message contained in the White Road wampum belt, and although it is direct and simple, as Crosslin states, such teachings "take hard work and dedication to apply to all that we say and do." They provide moral, ethical, and spiritual guidelines for how we treat each other, the land and waters, and our more-than-human plant and animal relatives. They also provide insight for how we acknowledge our connections to the past through our ancestors' spirits and our responsibilities to the future through those who have not yet come into this world.

In my reflections on these teachings and through incorporating them into my own life and work, their significance to how we view movements for social and environmental justice based on ethics of care and solidarity is profound. Further, the rich details that Crosslin offers for understanding and connecting to plants and animals as medicine, messengers, and teachers allows us to establish and refine these lessons in our approach to physical, mental, spiritual, and relational well-being. By sharing Keetoowah teachings, Crosslin helps us to see that our greatest mentors were placed here by the Creator, and that if we can honor them for the moral and relational guidance they provide, we might witness a decline in societal ills that currently plague the world - pollution and disease caused by the unbridled exploitation of the earth, systemic racism, and widespread psychological distress and alienation. When we view these ills as interconnected consequences of diverging from the White Path of *duyukdv* (**SGAᏛ**), it's not a far stretch to consider how Keetoowah Original Teachings offer us a way toward planetary health that includes solutions to our current climate crisis.

Crosslin is a spiritual leader grounded in tradition, place, and community; he is also worldly, educated, and a scholar of religious teachings. He is truly "in it" for everyone, and he offers up his services as a healer to anyone who might need them. His message of the need for spiritual unity among all people and the importance of community and mutual care is an urgent one today, when divisions among us run rampant and respect for one another and the earth is a secondary thought for many of the world's leaders. Crosslin understands that although the knowledge in this book and in *Stand as One* was entrusted to Keetoowahs as its guardians, the profound teachings they contain are for all humankind.

Although Crosslin is a remarkable person, it's hard to write about him solely as an individual - his family surrounds him with endless support and love. His wife of sixty-six years, Glenna, is a strong and proud Diné woman with thirty-five years of service to the Indian Health Service under her belt as a licensed practical nurse. Their children, Catherine, Junior, Kent, Caroline, and Geraldine, are all a part of this work in supporting and caring for their parents, and in modeling for their own children and grandchildren, nieces and nephews, the Keetoowah spirit.

I am forever grateful to be a part of ushering *Stand as One* and *Original Teachings* into the world. I hope they work to fulfill the ancestors' prayers that future generations of Cherokees can maintain and live these Keetoowah teachings, and that all people may draw from them in understanding their purpose in life and in honoring their gift of spirit from the Creator.

Clint Carroll
ᎤᎬᏍᏉᏧ ᏴᏝᏂᎰᏍᏉ
Longmont, Colorado
February 6, 2021

Reviews

Keetoowah Wisdom Channeled through Crosslin Smith

In our initiatives toward development in the medical, psychological, and social fields, we must be vigilant not to overlook the Wisdom Traditions too often assigned to irrelevant "pre-modern" knowledges. But some of us believe that the Wisdom Traditions offer lasting insights. Crosslin Smith's *Original Teachings* is filled with profound perspectives that offer knowledge about planes of awareness for personal exploration and teachings that address the deteriorating combative state of our contemporary society.

Earlier in his life, in the depths of despair, he was visited several times by a light that he believed to be God. The messages he received left no doubt that God exists and that there are realities outside our sense world. The primary message he received was that love unites everything, and it can be experienced on an emotional level and in acts of kindness. All his doubts were eclipsed, and he knew his destiny was to continue as a healer and to offer the message (which had been given to the Keetoowah centuries before) of goodness, hope, and love to people of all races.

Crosslin addresses one of the most discussed topics in Indian Country: that geographic genesis is intricately tied to tribal identity and that leaving one's homeland has detrimental effects upon one's tribal identity. The discussions often relate to the idea of tribal peoples' connections to the land they on which they were placed by God. One hears how our anxieties and fears are shaped by an area's weather, how work habits are associated with the resources of the land, and even the way one sees is conditioned by whether one occupies a wooded or a plains area.

Crosslin describes what the Keetoowah, who had lived in what is now North Carolina for 15,000 years, escaped war, disease, hunger, and strife brought with them in their flight to and settlement in Northeastern Oklahoma. Have these Oklahoma Indians lost their souls in their move? Crosslin does not argue with anyone. He essentially states that he still loves and honors the Keetoowah original homeland, and that the Keetoowahs brought the essence of their souls with them in the form of an Eternal Fire.

Keetoowahs knew they would be moving west long before it happened. It had been prophesied. They have kept the fire burning, embodying the core values and views given them by God. In a new homeland, Keetoowahs enact their tribal identities when they play traditional games in which they are taught not be angry with one another or jealous by playing in the spirit of integrity, humor, and congenial admiration. Before each Stickball game, Keetoowahs dance around the sacred fire on their ceremonial grounds, appreciating the Creator's blessings and increasing feelings of solidarity. Various other traditional games and ceremonies contribute to their sense of who they are as individuals and as a community. And they keep the Eternal Flame burning and protected by fire keepers.

In his day-to-day work as a healer Crosslin teaches that a vital aspect of healing is relationship building. He not only sees the importance of developing a relationship with his clients, but also with the plants and animals that he uses to facilitate the healings. Although he reveals his profound knowledge of the healing qualities and the applications of specific plants and animals, Crosslin's teachings are not simply operational. He also discusses the medicinal plants in the context of sick person's energy vibrations, and clients' feelings of self-worth. He also breaks down divisions that may separate animals and human beings, helping us to identify with animal characteristics, and encourages us to listen to them as teachers and advisors, so that we may recover a solidarity with the animal world that has been all but lost for most people.

Crosslin makes several points regarding community building that are of great value. First, he sees the Keetoowah people as a "chosen" community. This does not mean that there is no fragmentation within the community. It does mean that the Keetoowah represent an objective source of revelation with a message for the world. Crosslin meticulously describes its makeup of traditional Keetowah society, detailing its clan system and the role of elders. With his visionary insight, he illuminates the ceremonies that promote community cohesion, and the manifestation of love, despite its mistakes.

Crosslin's focus on his particular tribe has universal applications. He enumerates pitfalls that communities should avoid, as well as values they should express. He is especially emphatic about the dangers of disrespecting the leadership gifts of women and teaches that patriarchy as such can throw communities out of balance. In one of the few instances that he expresses distaste, he remarks how some tribal groups ostracize women from ceremonies and leadership positions. He encourages equality among all people and teaches that it is vital to approach each person with the knowledge that they possess divine gifts. He urges us to never act out of self-interest or "for show," but rather with the embodied intent to contribute to our larger communities. He writes, "Go out and help persons in need."

To conclude: to appreciate this book, one must be open to the deep subjective and inter-subjective dimensions of themselves and their connections with others. Crosslin bids us to explore our inner selves through meditative states where we can experience visions that point us to higher levels of awareness.

This review is an abstract review. To get the full weight of Crosslin's teachings, read his vision, which is clothed in stories, colors, drama, plants, and animals that open portals into other realms of reality where we can encounter the healing love of this great, but humble, Keetoowah medicine man.

Rockey Robbins, Ph.D.
Professor
Educational Psychology
University of Oklahoma

In 2009, a man by the name of James A. Ray, a New Age guru originally from Tulsa, Oklahoma, held a sweat lodge "ritual" for a large group of people who paid $250 apiece to take part in Ray's "Spirit Warrior Retreat." Three of the participants died as a result of the so-called ceremony which led to Ray's eventual incarceration for negligent homicide.

Shortly after the deaths occurred in Ray's "Spirit Warrior" sweat lodge, a local reporter contacted me to ask about these kinds of ceremonies and their significance in Native communities. In accordance with Western tradition, they contacted me as a professor in American Indian Studies rather than a Native medicine person, of whom there were several in or near Tucson, Arizona. I told this reporter that ceremonies are important to maintain our connections with one another and that every medicine person I have ever talked to told me that if you don't do these ceremonies correctly or with a *good heart* you might get someone hurt.

The messages that Ray and other New Age gurus send are starkly different from that of real medicine people and real chiefs like Crosslin Smith. Most importantly, the New Age gurus do not place an emphasis on an ethos of devotion toward others and the spirit of community. Theirs is a message of individualism and self-importance and even self-indulgence. Mr. Smith's newest book, *Original Teachings: Designed to Stand as One,* presents an opposing view. It seems that the focus of Cherokee knowledge is the maintenance of good and purposeful relationships with the earth, the spirit world, and other human beings.

In recent years, non-Indians, especially those in the media, have used the term "tribe" to describe extreme political partisanship. To them, tribalism is defined as a group of people who, more or less, live their lives hating other groups. Tribalism has been deemed exclusionary. Real tribalism, as Mr. Smith imparts, is inclusive because it is based on relationships. Smith uses the term "love" a great deal and it is essentially the way that human beings survive not as individuals in combat with the rest of the world, but rather as groups helping each other and sharing experiences together. In the early twentieth century, a Russian scientist named Peter Kropotkin wrote a book titled *Mutual Aid*. Kropotkin's thesis was that very many species, including human beings, evolved because of cooperation rather than individual competition and "survival of the fittest." It is indeed comforting to know, by way of Crosslin Smith's teachings, that

Cherokees and Indian people in general knew of mutual aid thousands of years before Kropotkin's hypothesis of human evolution.

The Keetoowah way is exactly the opposite of a western tradition that emphasizes disharmony, greed, and deception. In the tradition that Mr. Smith documents, the idea of having a respectful relationship with the natural world is inherent in the Cherokee language, the sacred history, the blessed elements of earth, wind, fire, and water, and the ceremonies performed to ensure the continuity of the Keetoowah ethos. The understanding that the world is alive is basic to that knowledge and to Mr. Smith's new book.

At this particular point in history, America is mired in racial, social, economic, and political divisions. In 1937, a book entitled *America Needs Indians!* was published. It remains relatively unknown, but its meaning was clear. It offered a message that the environment was in danger (even as early as the 1930s) and that the Native American ideas and spiritual knowledge would aid in rejuvenating an interest in conservation and harmony with the natural and spirit worlds. In 1973 Vine Deloria's book *God is Red* was released. Deloria made the point that American Indian beliefs were not only needed to heal the world, but necessary to understand the relations between human beings, the earth, and the cosmos, and that the extraordinary are real and very much in peril should we not change our ways of thinking and behaving. Crosslin Smith's two books, *Stand as One*, and this one, *Original Teachings*, drive home the notion that once again the world is in peril and that the ethos of the Keetoowah way offers a method of curing the illnesses caused by colonialism, rampant competition and consumerism, racial injustice, and ignoring the harm done to our environment.

Tom Holm, Ph.D.
Cherokee Nation Citizen
Professor Emeritus
American Indian Studies
University of Arizona

In his second book, respected Cherokee elder and spiritual leader, Crosslin Smith, offers more concepts, stories, and lessons meant to awaken the spirit given to all of us at birth by the Creator. His message originates from the Keetoowah Society, who are known as the keepers of the Eternal Flame and who live according to the old ways of the Cherokee people. Crosslin has lived his life based on these Original Teachings. He now invites us to read these stories and absorb their lessons to understand the spirit of goodness that resides within every one of us.

A traditional healer and counselor for all peoples, Crosslin presents these sacred teachings to the world in hopes of instilling a more harmonious life with the Earth and all the creations that dwell upon her. He stresses that the teachings and lessons contained herein are no longer the sole ownership of the Keetoowah Cherokees—they are, and have always been, universal truths for all peoples of the Earth.

Dr. Jody E. Noe, MS, ND
Natural Family Health & Integrative Medicine, LLC

Troubled by the corruption and erosion of respect for humankind and the Earth, Crosslin F. Smith has offered his second contribution to published indigenous wisdom traditions. He utilizes a coherent combination of Keetoowah/Cherokee oral teachings, cultural numerology, color symbolism, Biblical cross references, and personal history and spiritual testimony in recommending this strategy of cultural damage control in response to cultural loss and colonialism.

R. D. Theisz, Ph.D.
Professor Emeritus
English and Native American Studies
Black Hills State University

Original Teachings by Crosslin Smith appears to this reader as a memoir containing personal experiences, teachings, stories, and beliefs; philosophies of individual Cherokees; ceremonial and religious practices; and social mores of the Cherokee people. Much enlightening, educational, and historical information is shared. I find the information worthy of study. Anyone who makes the time to read and absorb Original Teachings will find him/herself fascinated.

Howard P. Bad Hand
Lakota Singer and Ceremonial Leader
Lead Singer of Heart Beat (formerly Red Leaf Takoja) Drum Group
Author of Native American Healing: A Lakota Ceremony

An Expanding Sphere of Keetoowah Influence

Crosslin Smith, known affectionately as "Grandpa" - a revered title among the Keetoowah - has been my teacher, mentor, elder, friend, and father figure since 1986, when he formally took me in as an apprentice in traditional medicine. Crosslin and his wife Glenna have been my parents in this way since I was 27 years old, and they are a formative part of my growth and training as an herbalist, doctor, healer, teacher, and human being. The teachings shared in this book are the most important lessons we can incorporate into the 21st century.

Dr. Jody E. Noe, MS, ND
Natural Family Health & Integrative Medicine, LLC

Love and care for oneself and all people - *adagesdi*. This sacred concept epitomizes the life of Crosslin Smith.

When this concept speaks of caring for oneself, it speaks more than just caring for your personal well-being, but it is requiring that you ar right with the Creator and with all of our Keetoowah traditional ways. The ways that Crosslin so eloquently describes and teaches in his first book *Stand as One* and followed now by *Original Teachings*. He is inviting us to open ourselves to this realm of our traditional ways that have been taught to only a few. Knowing that those few have dwindled over the years, he knew one day that he may be the only one left to pass these wonderful teachings on.

Original Teachings is not a book that you pick up, read and move on. It is a book that you keep close to you to remind yourself to keep our traditional ways daily. You and I must be responsible for passing those on to our youth or they will truly become just a myth, something somewhere long ago that people use to believe. As you are equipped to spiritually take care of yourself and are steadfast in keeping the traditional ways then you are then prepared to care for others.

Crosslin was chosen for this Spiritual path, he responded to his calling with an open heart and received the teachings from his father, Stokes and his grandfather Redbird Smith.

My family has known the Smith family for many years. When my oldest sister was three years old, she was stricken with polio. Living in the hills of Vian, Oklahoma where so many were dirt poor, getting to a medical doctor was not easily done and for our Cherokees generally not sought after.

The first person my family contacted was our traditional healer, Stokes Smith. Stokes told my Mom and Dad, "You have to believe that the Creator is going to use me to help her or what I do will do no good!" My parents are full-blood Cherokee, fluent Cherokee speakers and know the traditional Keetoowah ways. Of course, they believed.

Stokes stayed in our home day and night for months. He built a fire and every morning he went to the Creek to go to water to spend time with the Creator "caring for himself" and to gather the medicines of roots and plants that he needed to care for my sister. Today, after forty years as a nurse, she recently retired. She was taught by example of love and care for herself and for others. We now have five members of our immediate family who have chosen nursing as their careers.

Crosslin is a treasure. I am so proud to know he and his family. He reminds us to "renew our love and the Creator's Spirit in us and to become one with love and spirit, body and soul …and do this in the right state of mind and then we become one with the loving spirit of God!"

Linda Leaf Bolin
Director of Indian Education Author of Children's Native Books
Founder of Greater Tulsa Cherokees Community

Creek "Ma-Ga-Yi" McCoy was born in the 1820s in Coosewata, Georgia.Like many Cherokees, he moved to the "Cherokee Nation West," located in what is now the State of Oklahoma. There, according to the 1851 Drennen Roll, he lived in the Illinois District until he died sometime after 1880. He married his third wife, "We-Ti-Yah," or "Oo-Ti-Ye," Proctor, who also was from Georgia, in 1854. They had one child, a boy, Alexander McCoy, born in 1855.

Alexander McCoy, also known as "Big Alex," and "Old Alec" McCoy, lived in what is now Sequoyah County, Oklahoma. He ran a trading post near the McCoy Stomp Grounds. He was an active member of the Keetoowah Society that is the traditional spiritual social order of the Cherokees, the one that maintains an identity separate from the political leadership and entities of the Nation.

Old Alec's seventh wife was Saphronia Lee. They had nine children, including Lilah "Lillie" McCoy, who was born in 1885. Lilah McCoy married Stoke Smith, whose family also was involved in the spiritual Keetoowah Society. Lilah and Stoke Smith had eight children, including Crosslin Smith. Alec McCoy is my Great-Grandfather. Many thanks to Jimmie and Jeri McCoy who researched and published the McCoy genealogy in 2006.

I understand, from my ancestors, and from those living Cherokees that have taught me, including Crosslin, the importance of knowledge. I understand from my decades of interactions with other Indigenous Peoples, through family, through friendship, and through my work as an attorney at the Native American Rights Fund, that many Indigenous Peoples around the world believe that our knowledge comes from the Creator.

The knowledge, like many things, is eternal, but the Creator decides what living beings, including humans, get what knowledge, its meaning, and whether and how to use it. And so, I am grateful - *wado* - to the Creator for entrusting Crosslin with the knowledge that he has. And I am grateful - *wado* - for Crosslin and for all those who teach the knowledge with the utmost respect for it.

Melody McCoy
Boulder, Colorado
March 8, 2021

I first met Crosslin Smith in the early 1980s, when I was serving as principal of the Cherokee Nation alternative school. Crosslin and I soon formed a friendship, and he has been a cherished mentor to me ever since. One day, I sought Crosslin's counsel about an impactful dream that had come to me years prior. His interpretation of that dream set me on a path working with Native youth to instill confidence and positive leadership traits. He explained to me that in receiving that dream, "this is what you're being asked to do."

In 1982, not long after Crosslin's interpretation, I founded Project Venture, a positive youth development program for American Indian, Alaska Native, and Indigenous Pacific Island youth. The program evolved as a synthesis of Crosslin's traditional teachings, combined with my outdoor adventure background and experience as a teacher and principal of tribal schools. The program has its roots in the Cherokee Nation, where we conducted the first leadership camp in 1983. The camp model was redesigned in the mid-1980s into its current form—a year-round program for middle and high school youth that features in-school and after-school activities, multi-day trips and expeditions, summer camps, and a year-long curriculum. Crosslin's emphasis on positivity in all interactions with young people serves as the foundational principle for our work.

Today, Project Venture is internationally recognized and is the evidence-based flagship program of the National Indian Youth Leadership Project. Our program has been recognized by the Substance Abuse Mental Health Services Administration, the U.S. Department of Health and Human Services, and the Center for Substance Abuse Prevention as a Model Program, indicating that it consistently achieves the highest level of effectiveness in meeting its goals.

In 2002, the National High Risk Youth Study identified Project Venture as the "Most Effective Program" serving American Indian/Alaska Native youth. The Director of the study, Dr. Fred Springer, found that our program contained all eight components identified as the characteristics of the most effective programs he had studied. From there, Project Venture went on to receive "Exemplary" and "Promising" designations. Finally, in 2005, we received the "Model Program" designation. Project Venture is the first Native-developed program to achieve this status. As a result of this success, Project Venture has been replicated in over twenty-five U.S. states (including Hawaii, working with Native Hawaiian youth), nine Canadian provinces, and in Hungary, where it was adapted for Romani youth.

The program's success is owed in large part to the mentorship Crosslin has provided in its 38 years of existence. Many of the cultural and spiritual teachings that Crosslin shares in this book guide our collaborative work as a team of Native educators who seek to model and instill in young people positive behaviors and healthy lifestyles. Crosslin has been the spiritual advisor to Project Venture since its inception and we are greatly indebted to this highly regarded Cherokee elder and spiritual leader of the Keetoowah tradition.

For more information on this program, please visit www.ProjectVenture.org and the National Indian Youth Leadership Project Facebook page.

McClellan Hall, MA
Founder and CEO, National Indian Youth Leadership Project
Executive Director, Project Venture

About the Author

Crosslin Fields Smith was born November 27, 1929 to a traditional Keetoowah family. The members of the Keetoowah Society are best known as the keepers of God's Eternal Flame. He is the son of Stokes Smith, and grandson of Redbird Smith who is the modern-day founder of the Keetoowah Society.

When he was a boy, Crosslin attended Indian School at Dwight Mission, in Vian, Oklahoma. Later, as a teenager, he attended Chilocco Indian Boarding School. During the four years he served in the 45th Division of the Oklahoma National Guard in the Korean War, President Truman activated the Guard; they served fourteen months in Korea with the 279th Infantry Regiment.

After his military service, he attended Northeastern State University in Tahlequah, Oklahoma, graduating in 1957 with a BS in Education and holds both elementary and secondary education teaching certificates from the state of Oklahoma. In 2019, he received an Honorary Degree of Doctor of Humane Letters from Bacone College in Muskogee, Oklahoma. Formal education has always been important to Crosslin and his family.

Crosslin is now retired from a thirty-year career of civil service. He states that he has always represented the Cherokee Nation. He is the first employee of the Cherokee Nation - from 1964 to the present - as a spiritual resource person. He has worked under Chiefs W.W. Keeler, Ross Swimmer, Wilma Mankiller, Bill John Baker, and the present Chuck Hoskin Jr. During the reorganization of the Cherokee Nation in the 1960s, Crosslin served as a U.S. liaison officer to his Cherokee people and was responsible for informing them on the status of negotiations between the tribe and the U.S. government.

Through the years, he became the tribe's spiritual practitioner, performing blessings at official functions and at the start of new tribal development projects. In 2013, he was honored by his people with the Cherokee National Statesman Award. In 2014, Smith was among seven Cherokees honored at the AARP Oklahoma Indian Elder Honors event for their impact on their tribes and communities. In 2020, Crosslin was recognized by the Cherokee Nation as a Cherokee National Treasure.

A noted keynote and university lecturer, Crosslin has standing engagements in the United States and abroad. He states, "With the highest diplomatic credit and character, I have worked to build a Cherokee Nation for the Cherokee people. I fought in the Korean War. In this war, I represented the U.S. government and the American system. In all of my efforts, I worked to part of the system instead of against it." As a spiritual leader and wisdom keeper for the Cherokee Nation, he also gives a traditional blessing and prayer at the annual State of the Union address for the current principal chief and administration.

Crosslin and his wife Glenna live in Vian, Oklahoma, surrounded by their many children, grandchildren, and great-grandchildren.

www.ingramcontent.com/pod-product-compliance
Lightning Source LLC
Chambersburg PA
CBHW072205100526
44589CB00015B/2376
9781737136224